# EDUCATION ON THE INTERNET

# THE WORLDWIDE CLASSROOM
Access to People, Resources, and
Curricular Connections

*2003 Update*

Peggy A. Ertmer

Carole Hruskocy

Denise M. Woods

Merrill
Prentice Hall

Upper Saddle River, New Jersey
Columbus, Ohio

Vice President and Publisher: Jeffery W. Johnston
Executive Editor: Debra A. Stollenwerk
Editorial Assistant: Mary Morrill
Production Editor: Kris Robinson
Design Coordinator: Diane C. Lorenzo
Cover Designer: Ali Mohrman
Production Manager: Pam Bennett
Director of Marketing: Ann Castel Davis
Marketing Manager: Amy June
Marketing Coordinator: Tyra Poole

Pearson Education Ltd.
Pearson Education Australia Pty. Limited
Pearson Education Singapore Pte. Ltd.
Pearson Education North Asia Ltd.
Pearson Education Canada, Ltd.
Pearson Educación de Mexico, S.A. de C.V.
Pearson Education—Japan
Pearson Education Malaysia Pte. Ltd.
Pearson Education, *Upper Saddle River, New Jersey*

Earlier editions of this work were written by Andrew T. Stull
(first edition) and Randall J. Ryder (second edition).

---

10 9 8 7 6 5 4 3 2

Merrill
Prentice Hall

ISBN: 0-13-112638-5

## TRADEMARK INFORMATION:

*Netscape Navigator* is a registered trademark of Netscape Communications Corporation. *Internet Explorer* is a registered trademark of Microsoft Corporation.

# CONTENTS

# PREFACE

Welcome to the *WorldWide Classroom*, a quick and easy guide to using the Internet in your classroom. As you may have already discovered, there is a wealth of information available on the Internet. Access to this information can transform classrooms into WorldWide Classrooms, teeming with rich and abundant information resources. But these transformations don't occur just because schools and classrooms are connected to the Internet. Rather, a WorldWide Classroom evolves as educators learn to integrate Internet resources into meaningful curricular-based learning experiences. With this text as your guide, we expect that you, too, will begin the transformation process—using worldwide resources to create rich learning experiences for your students.

## Who Should Use This Book?

This book is designed for both current and future teachers. Whether you are located in a public or private school, urban or rural setting, an elementary or secondary classroom, this book will help you access the Internet in ways that meet the needs of you *and* your students. Without getting too technical, we will help you understand just enough about how the Internet works so that you can find and use the resources that are available on the Internet. In addition we will describe how you can use the Internet to meet the technology standards for teachers (NETS*T) established by the International Society for Technology in Education (ISTE).

## What Resources are Within the *WorldWide Classroom*?

The Internet can help you meet both professional and instructional goals. For example, in this guide you will learn how to:

- achieve ISTE NETS*T standards through meaningful uses of the Internet
- connect with experts in your field
- join educational listservs
- participate in teacher chats

- conduct effective Internet searches
- create your own web pages
- locate web sites relevant to specific content needs

All of these topics address your professional needs. In addition, you will learn how to use these same Internet tools to create instructional activities that enable your students to:

- interact with experts
- collaborate with students and teachers around the world
- participate in local and global projects
- publish original work
- achieve national and state content standards
- evaluate the accuracy, credibility, and relevancy of web site information

By addressing your professional *and* instructional needs in this book, we provide the tools you need to keep your own skills honed while simultaneously bringing your students up-to-speed.

## What's New in This Edition?

The Internet has grown considerably since this book was first published. The number of users has increased exponentially, not only in English-speaking countries, but globally as well. It is estimated that by 2005, one billion people from around the world will be connected to the Internet. Connection speeds have increased, as has the ability to send and receive all kinds of multimedia data, including video and audio streams.

As much as possible, the current edition of the *WorldWide Classroom* reflects these changes in Internet capability and access. In addition, we include information on topics about which teachers continue to ask (e.g., assessment techniques, copyright laws). For example, in this edition you will find new information about:

- ISTE technology standards for teachers (NETS*T)
- WebQuests
- Rubrics
- Web-based video conferencing

2

- Instant messaging
- Online journals
- Copyright and privacy laws

## How is This Book Organized?

If we had to describe the Internet in one word, that word would be *access*. We believe that the true power of the Internet lies in the access that it provides to people, resources, and ideas. This is why we organized this text around this theme. Thus, Chapters 2 through 5 each deal with a particular type of access that the Internet affords (access to people, resources, etc.), while the last chapter deals with issues related to having Internet access (safety, equity, etc.).

There are a variety of Internet services available, each serving a different educational purpose. In this text, we look specifically at using the Internet as:

- a communication tool
- a tutoring/mentoring tool
- a teaching/learning resource
- a publishing house

The first two applications connect us to *people*. The second two connect us to *resources*. Chapters 2 and 3 describe how to use the Internet for these purposes.

In addition, the Internet has become a gold mine of teaching ideas, strategies, and lesson plans. Chapters 4 and 5 direct you to resources that can help you integrate the Internet into your curriculum in meaningful ways.

Finally, in the last chapter, we address issues related to Internet access: equity, safety, and responsibility. As with many valuable resources, the Internet is not completely risk-free. Both students and teachers need to be aware of potential problems and to practice thoughtful and responsible use.

NOTE: Due to the changing nature of the Internet, the sites listed in this text may have moved, changed, or been deleted by the time of publication!

# CHAPTER 1
## INTRODUCTION

Although it is probably beneficial to know a little bit about the history of the Internet (it began about 30 years ago), to be able to define it (a worldwide collection, or network, of millions of computers linked together), and to be able to distinguish it from the World Wide Web (an Internet service that supports multimedia and consists of a collection of linked documents), this information does not go very far to support your teaching or your students' learning. We believe that the most important thing you need to know about the Internet is *how to use it!* And along with that, you need to know how to help your students use it as a tool to achieve meaningful outcomes.

Like many others, we believe that the primary goal of education is to engage students in meaningful learning. According to Jonassen, Peck, and Wilson (1999), this includes helping students:

- recognize and solve problems
- comprehend new phenomena
- construct mental models of those phenomena
- set goals and regulate their own learning within each learning situation (p. 7)

While the Internet can be used for many other purposes, this text stresses using the Internet in ways that will facilitate students' accomplishment of the four goals listed above.

Together, the Internet and the World Wide Web have the potential to change the way we teach and learn. Yet the potential lies not in the amount of information that we can access, but in the way in which both teachers and students *interact* with that information. If we use the Internet primarily as an information resource (much like a library), then much of its potential remains untapped. For it is through the Internet's interactive capability that we are able to extend and transform the intellectual activity in our classrooms. The Internet makes it both possible and exciting to interact with others, with oral and visual information, and with scientific data.

Because of this interactivity, our intellectual world can extend far beyond the traditional classroom walls.

Jonassen et al. (1999) noted: "The Internet can immerse students in stimulating, challenging, motivating, and vibrant learning environments that provide a context in which computer literacy develops—not as a goal, but as a requirement in order to achieve much higher goals" (p. 20). These higher goals relate to the skills and qualities that will be expected of all students in the future: creative thinking, problem solving, cooperation, independence, and self-discipline, to name a few. In this book, we help you think about how to facilitate these engaging types of uses, as well as point you to relevant web sites that will get you started.

## How Can I Meet Content and Technology Standards Through Use of the Internet?

In Chapter 4 of this text, you will find Internet addresses (URLs) for the national professional organizations in math, science, social studies, English/language arts, art, music, and physical education. These organizations publish content standards for K-12 students and also include, among their lists, standards related to technology. The web sites featured in Chapters 4 and 5 contain resources that you can use to help your students meet the various content standards for each grade level.

In addition, the International Society for Technology in Education (ISTE) has developed National Educational Technology Standards for both students (NET*S) and teachers (NETS*T) (see http://www.iste.org for more information). Since the content of this text is directed primarily toward teachers, we continually refer to the NETS*T standards throughout the book in order to highlight the specific standards being addressed by the different topics. For ease of reference, we also list the standards here.

### What are the ISTE Technology Standards for Teachers?[*]

The ISTE NETS*T comprise six broad areas of technology competency:

- Technology operations and concepts
- Planning and designing learning environments and experiences
- Teaching, learning, and the curriculum
- Assessment and evaluation
- Productivity and professional practice
- Social, ethical, legal, and human issues

Each main competency area includes two to five specific indicators that describe how teachers can demonstrate achievement of the standards. These are included below.

I. **Technology Operations and Concepts:** Teachers demonstrate a sound understanding of technology operations and concepts. Teachers
   A. demonstrate introductory knowledge, skills, and understanding of concepts related to technology
   B. demonstrate continual growth in technology, knowledge, and skills to stay abreast of current and emerging technologies

II. **Planning and Designing Learning Environments and Experiences:** Teachers plan and design effective learning environments and experiences supported by technology. Teachers
   A. design developmentally appropriate learning opportunities that apply technology-enhanced instructional strategies to support the diverse needs of learners
   B. apply current research on teaching and learning with technology when planning learning environments and experiences
   C. identify and locate technology resources and evaluate them for accuracy and suitability
   D. plan for the management of technology resources within the context of learning activities
   E. plan strategies to manage student learning in a technology-enhanced environment

III. **Teaching, Learning, and the Curriculum:** Teachers implement curriculum plans that include methods and strategies for applying technology to maximize student learning.

Teachers

A. facilitate technology-enhanced experiences that address content standards and student technology standards
B. use technology to support learner-centered strategies that address the diverse needs of students
C. apply technology to develop students' higher-order skills and creativity
D. manage student learning activities in a technology-enhanced environment

IV. **Assessment and Evaluation:** Teachers apply technology to facilitate a variety of effective assessment and evaluation strategies.

Teachers

A. apply technology in assessing student learning of subject matter using a variety of assessment techniques
B. use technology resources to collect and analyze data, interpret results, and communicate findings to improve instructional practice and maximize student learning
C. apply multiple methods of evaluation to determine students' appropriate use of technology resources for learning, communication, and productivity

V. **Productivity and Professional Practice:** Teachers use technology to enhance their productivity and professional practice.

Teachers

A. use technology resources to engage in ongoing professional development and lifelong learning
B. continually evaluate and reflect on professional practice to make informed decisions regarding the use of technology in support of student learning
C. apply technology to increase productivity
D. use technology to communicate and collaborate with peers, parents, and the larger community in order to nurture student learning

VI. **Social, Ethical, Legal, and Human Issues:** Teachers understand the social, ethical, legal, and human issues surrounding the use of technology in PK-12 schools and apply that understanding in practice.

Teachers
A.  model and teach legal and ethical practice related to technology use
B.  apply technology resources to enable and empower learners with diverse backgrounds, characteristics, and abilities
C.  identify and use technology resources that affirm diversity
D.  promote safe and healthy use of technology resources
E.  facilitate equitable access to technology resources

## *Summary*

The great news about the Internet is that it provides you with almost limitless amounts of up-to-date information. The bad news is that it provides you with almost limitless amounts of up-to-date information. Teachers are too busy to sort through all of this information in order to find the perfect site for tomorrow's science lesson. This text eliminates much of the sorting process (we've done it for you) so you can locate and implement powerful lessons for your students today. Whether you teach in a kindergarten classroom or a high school chemistry classroom, this text will serve as an excellent resource for both you and your students.

We hope that you enjoy your journey!

## *References*

Jonassen, D. H., Peck, K. L., & Wilson, B. G. (1999). *Learning with technology: A constructivist perspective.* Upper Saddle River, NJ: Prentice Hall/Merrill.

# CHAPTER 2
## ACCESS TO PEOPLE

*ISTE NETS V: Teachers use technology to enhance their productivity and professional practice.*

The Internet and World Wide Web open up numerous channels of communication for both teachers and students. Once connected, the possibilities for sending and receiving information are many. Communication is enhanced through the use of the Internet when:

- colleagues communicate with colleagues
- professionals from around the world share ideas
- teachers communicate with their students
- students converse with diverse populations across the globe

This section is organized into two parts. The first part introduces common ways to send and receive messages via the Internet including:

- email
- chat rooms
- instant messages
- discussion groups
- listservs
- threaded discussion boards
- newsgroups
- forums
- collaborative workspaces
- web-based video conferencing

The second part introduces the use of the Web for tutoring or mentoring. There are several web sites that connect the user to "experts" who may provide help by answering questions or assisting on projects. These web sites are commonly called:

- telementoring
- "ask an expert"

Teachers and students can benefit from the variety of communication channels available through the Web. An abundance of information and ready resources become accessible with one click of the mouse. Classrooms can be transformed as teachers and students establish worldwide connections.

## What is Email?

"Email" stands for electronic mail. With email, a letter or message is sent from one person to another but without the help of the post office; instead, the written message is sent across the phone lines, from one computer to another. Without even picking up the phone, your email message is sent to the intended receiver.

Both sender and receiver benefit from the convenience and ease of electronic mail. Email has become a common mode of communication because messages can be:

- immediately sent and received anywhere in the world
- delivered to any number of people at once
- sent according to the sender's time schedule
- delivered even if the receiver's phone line is busy
- accessed according to the receiver's schedule

Although email has quickly become a popular form of communication, users should proceed with caution. Your email remarks are not truly private. Email can be read by systems administrators or by your email provider. Messages that you send privately can be forwarded to (and edited by) others without your knowledge or permission.

### *What does an email address look like?*

An email address consists of four main parts:
- the user ID
- the "at" sign
- the domain name
- the extension

For example, an email address might look like this:

johndoe@mabell.gov

- the user ID = johndoe
- the "at" sign = @
- the domain name = mabell
- the extension = gov

The user ID is often the user's name. The "at" sign (@) always precedes the domain name. The domain name is the Internet server that houses the person's email account or the organization that provides your account (and for which you typically pay a monthly fee). The domain name is usually followed by the extension that signifies the type of organization sponsoring the account. Common extensions include *edu* for educational organizations, *gov* for government accounts, *com* for commercial organizations, and *net* for network providers.

You use a personal password to access your email account. Together, you and your service provider will set up your email account and password. Some tips for protecting your account and ensuring the confidentiality of your password include:

- using an uncommon password
  (avoid using your name, birth date, etc.)
- using a combination of numbers and letters
- changing your password often

### What are chat rooms and instant messages?

Most Internet services provide their users with the ability to talk in real time with each other through the use of *chat rooms* and *instant messages (IM)*. A chat room allows a group of people to type in messages that are seen by everyone in the "room," while instant messages are basically a chat room for two people. Instant messaging allows you to maintain a list of people with whom you wish to interact. You can send messages to any person on your list, often called a buddy or contact list, as long as that person is online. Sending a message opens up a small window in which you and your friend can type messages that both of you can see.

# How Can I Use Email for Professional Purposes?

Email offers many conveniences and saves time and energy. Messages to colleagues in the same building or school district can be sent and received right from your desk, including:

- reminders of meetings
- questions about needed resources
- messages concerning students or parents
- notes on school events

Once connected to the Internet, you can email colleagues outside of the school system. Vast arrays of resources are now at your fingertips as you begin communicating with a variety of teachers on educational issues such as lesson planning, classroom management, and technology implementation.

Besides traditional email, many Internet web sites can connect you to resources that lead to email communications with online experts and classrooms around the world. Both you and your students can benefit from the connections listed below.

**AskERIC**
http://askeric.org/Qa/

*AskERIC* is an Internet-based service that provides educational information to teachers, administrators, and parents, throughout the United States and around the world. It began as a project of the ERIC Clearinghouse on Information and Technology at Syracuse University. It contains the resources of the entire ERIC system and has a service in which you can ask educational questions of a staff of researchers. To ask a question, email askeric@askeric.org.

**Teachnet**
http://www.teachnet.com/t2t/

*Teachnet* keeps you connected with educators around the world for free! There are three different ways you can stay connected—daily email, daily email digest, or weekly announcements. This list focuses on the exchange of ideas relevant to preK-12 classrooms. Professional conversations and the sharing of lesson plans and teaching tips are part of the wide range of discussions at this site.

## How Can I Use Email for Instructional Purposes?

The Internet allows you to connect students with other students around the world. By connecting with other classrooms, unique projects or programs can be developed to:

- enhance the curriculum
- establish new friendships
- enrich student communication skills

Some suggested activities to get you and your students connected around the world include:

- researching another classroom's city, state, or country
- collecting and sharing data on a common curricular project
- establishing a database of contacts around the world
- collaborating on story writing
- exchanging pictures of local landmarks and historical figures
- sharing journal entries noting similarities and differences
- linking older and younger students via mentoring experiences

Visit the addresses below to find schools connected to the Internet.

**Intercultural E-mail Classroom Connections (IECC)**
http://www.iecc.org/

*IECC* is a free teaching.com service to help teachers link with partners in other cultures and countries for email classroom pen pals and other project exchanges. Since its creation in 1992, *IECC* has distributed over 28,000 requests for email partnerships.

**ePALS**
http://www.epals.com/

*ePALS* is the world's largest online classroom community and leading provider of student-safe email. At registration there are four audiences from which to select—teachers, students, parents,

13

higher education. Once registered, teachers and students can communicate electronically with other classrooms around the world.

***Besides email, how can I communicate through the Internet?***

Besides the basic, personal email message between two people, there are various other techniques that allow for electronic communication between individuals or groups. These techniques have an assortment of names that may vary according to the resource you consult. The most common names include:

- mailing lists
- discussion groups
- listservs
- threaded discussion boards
- newsgroups
- forums
- bulletin boards
- collaborative work spaces
- web-based video conferencing

Mailing lists and discussion group messages are emailed to individual subscribers. They are often referred to as listservs. Threaded discussion occurs among a group of people posting messages to a common software program. Newsgroups and forums are messages posted on an electronic bulletin board for anyone to read and answer. They may also be called bulletin boards or "BBS" (bulletin board service).

Authors and Internet users often interchange these terms. Thus, for the average Internet user, understanding the technical differences between these terms is often confusing. Basically, they are all types of electronic communication that connect you with a variety of people and resources around the world.

A new set of options has surfaced recently that provide additional methods of electronic communication and collaboration, including collaborative workspaces and web-based video conferencing. They are described in more detail later in this chapter.

# What are Mailing Lists, Discussion Groups, and Threaded Discussion Boards?

A *mailing list* allows an individual to send email to multiple recipients at the same time. A mailing list requires the user to subscribe in order to send and receive such messages. The first subscription mailing list administered by a computer was a program called LISTSERV; thus, "mailing list" and "listserv" are often used synonymously.

When using a mailing list, you first send email to the designated mailing list address. The message is then automatically copied and sent to all other subscribed members. This method is especially useful when sharing information with a group and can be done through either a private or public listserv. Private listservs restrict membership to certain groups such as people working together on committees or a group of college classmates.

Mailing lists and discussion groups may both be referred to as listservs, but they differ slightly. With mailing lists, a single person produces messages for distribution to subscribers. In contrast, discussion groups resemble conversation among many people on a common topic. Anyone can contribute a message that all members receive. Some discussion groups are open; some require membership. Users join discussion groups with the specific intent of requesting or offering information about a set topic.

Discussion groups are often affiliated with academic organizations. Teachers may connect to discussion groups based on individual interests or geographical regions such as special education, science, language arts, or the Midwest. Discussion groups can provide valuable links to professional colleagues around the world.

A threaded discussion board is similar to a discussion group, but requires all participants to have access to the same software program. Once logged onto the program, a threaded discussion board becomes an informal meeting place where the members of a class can share ideas and comments. Like a physical meeting, members of the group listen to what others have to say and can voice their own opinions. However, unlike a physical meeting, the members do not have to be in the same room at the same time to share information. With access to the Internet and a software program, people can participate anywhere, anytime.

Threaded discussion boards are a fantastic way to facilitate online discussions and have become popular for use in college courses. With this technology, you and your students have the ability to communicate with one another without coordinating your schedules. Plus, your email inbox will not overflow with a large number of messages that may be generated through the use of an email discussion list. There are many threaded discussion applications on the market such as Lotus Notes or Digiposts. You can visit their web sites at http://lotusnotes.com/home.nsf or http://digiposts.com/.

Mailing lists, discussion groups, and threaded discussion boards offer asynchronous communication; that is, the sender leaves a message to be read at the receiver's convenience. Synchronous communication, where the sender and receiver participate in a real-time conversation, is also possible through the Internet. This form of communication, described in the first part of this chapter, is commonly referred to as a "chat channel" or "chat room" that allows the sender and receiver to "chat" in real time.

The following web site can connect you with several mailing lists or provide opportunities to chat with students around the world.

**Kidlink**
http://www.kidlink.org/

*Kidlink* offers a network of mailing lists and real-time interactions for both teachers and students. At this site, participants can link with people from a variety of countries for conversation and sharing. Online activities are also available in many different languages. Participation is for all students through secondary school.

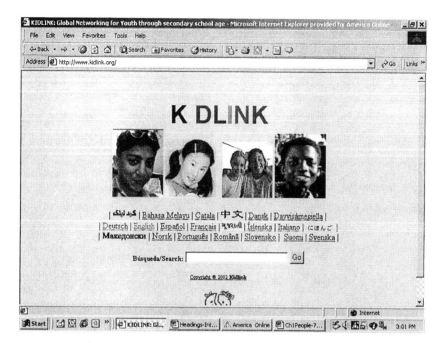

### *How do I subscribe to a listserv?*

Sign-up procedures for each listserv will vary, but generally you send an email message to the address of the list manager. The procedure is simple and requires little time. A typical subscribe message is typed in the body of the email text and looks like this:

Subscribe listname firstname lastname

An example might be:

Subscribe EDCI564 carole hruskocy

This message assures that Carole Hruskocy is signed onto the EDCI 564 class mailing list and can communicate with her students by using one common email address.

17

Typically, listservs follow these procedures for subscribing:

- email your message to the listserv address
- leave the subject line blank
- write the subscribe message in the body of the email
- remove any "signature blocks" at the end of your email

Most listservs send you a message confirming your membership. Once you are registered, you will receive many messages from other listserv members. Just remember that any message you send to the list will be viewed by all members of that listserv. You have the option to unsubscribe at any point in time. Instructions are usually provided in the original confirmation message.

## What are Newsgroups and Forums?

This type of electronic communication differs from the traditional mailing list and discussion group listserv because messages are not delivered to your personal electronic mailbox. Users must visit a particular web site to read and post messages.

Newsgroups and forums offer additional ways of collaborating on the Internet. Like listservs, they provide an arena for sharing similar interests or discussing related topics. Global communication is enhanced as users share their thoughts and ideas on subjects of mutual interest and concern.

Unlike listserv participants, newsgroup and forum participants do not have to sign up or subscribe. Messages are posted on an electronic bulletin board. Individuals may visit the bulletin board to look for messages of interest and to post replies. Anyone can search the Web and join these discussions.

Because these bulletin boards are accessible to every Internet user, the level of discussion can vary from highly intellectual to unenlightened. Some newsgroups and forums are moderated for content but discussion is usually uncensored. Users may be exposed to a wide variety of beliefs, which may differ radically from their own. Participants should be aware of the open nature of newsgroup and forum conversations and proceed with caution.

# What are Collaborative Workspaces and Web-Based Video Conferencing?

Two recent developments in electronic communication include collaborative workspaces and web-based video conferencing. Each offers a unique method for sharing data or information among participants.

*Collaborative workspaces* refer to files or folders on a computer network that provide a common area for people to work electronically. To help collaboration, all members of a group have access to the same files and folders. Thus, each member of the group can use this space to share work and information with the other members. These workspaces might help a group of students share ideas about a group project. Or a teacher and student might exchange assignments and feedback through a shared workspace.

One of the most recent developments in electronic communication is *web-based video conferencing*. Also called a classroom conference, this form of virtual communication is a meeting conducted over the Internet in which the participants can see and hear each other, even though the attendees might be in different places. Teachers can sit in their own classrooms and present a "live" lecture in front of a camera attached to a web server. Using a simple switching device and several cameras, the teacher can provide remote participants with graphics, sound, and visual aids. This type of communication uses video conferencing software such as CUseeMe or NetMeeting to connect communities, cultures, and classrooms so students around the world can learn and collaborate together. Students can use live conferencing to share research results, interact with experts, and practice speaking different languages.

These sites provide more information on classroom conferencing.

**CUseeMe (First Virtual's Click to Meet Web Conferencing)**
http://www.cuseeme.com/about/index.htm

This site features First Virtual Communications web-based technologies including CUseeMe and other conferencing products.

**Microsoft's NetMeeting**
http://www.microsoft.com/windows/netmeeting/

The NetMeeting home page offers information on Microsoft products specific to web conferencing.

**Global SchoolNet**
http://www.gsn.org/cu/index.html

This site provides a classroom conference directory to help find other schools, worldwide, that use video conferencing. You can list your school in their directory or join a video conference discussion list to let others know that you are available to video conference.

## How Can I Use Electronic Communication for Professional Purposes?

Listservs and bulletin boards can connect you to professionals around the world. By subscribing to a listserv, you'll be able to participate in professional discussions on a variety of topics such as those listed below. By connecting to a bulletin board, you'll access a variety of thoughts on a selected topic and may add your own ideas as well. Common themes include:

- national and state curricular standards
- curricular requirements and activities
- discipline techniques
- classroom management
- technology integration
- professional development
- restructuring and school change

Several listservs, specific to the use of the Internet and educational technology, are provided below. Today most listserv web sites provide a direct link that allows you to subscribe. Some listservs still require that you subscribe by sending an email message directly to the listserv. An example of how to subscribe is provided along with a web site that explains how to unsubscribe to a list.

**EDTECH**
This discussion list centers on issues related to educational

technology. To subscribe, address an email message in the following manner:

(send the message to)
listserv@msu.edu
(in the body of the message type)
Subscribe EDTECH firstname lastname

## Publicly Accessible Mailing Lists
http://paml.net/gettingoff.html

This web site provides detailed instructions for how to unsubscribe from a listserv. A mailing list directory, including an index of listservs, can also be found at this site.

Because there is a vast array of mailing lists, discussion groups, newsgroups, and forums available on the Internet, locating appropriate groups may be difficult and time consuming. There are a number of web sites that simplify this process by providing indexes of available listservs. These addresses might be a good place to start your search for online professional discussions.

## Listservs—Resource Page for Technology Coordinators
http://www.maderacoe.k12.ca.us/tech/listserv.html

This web site includes links to email discussion lists, electronic journals, listservs, and newsgroups related to instructional technology, and a collection of educational listservs related to a variety of topics.

## Voices of Youth Website
http://www.unicef.org/voy/index.html

Sponsored by United Nations Children's Fund (UNICEF), this web site offers three forums. Teachers and students can express views on current global issues or participate in online learning projects.

## Teachers Helping Teachers
http://www.pacificnet.net/~mandel/

This web site is the home page by teachers, for teachers. *Teachers*

*Helping Teachers* is an online network of teachers sharing ideas about classroom management, special education, and every subject area in the K-12 curriculum. A teacher forum is available to post questions and comments.

## School.Net
http://www.k12.school.net/go/forums/

*SchoolNet* provides online discussion groups for teachers, students, parents, and others interested in education. Forums are organized by subject area, educational topics, and peer groups. Some educational groups have their own specific forums.

## How Can I Use Electronic Communication for Instructional Purposes?

With the help of the World Wide Web, students can interact with others outside of the local learning community on a daily basis. Listservs and bulletin boards can enhance the classroom curriculum and enrich students' learning experiences. Through these Internet exchanges students can:

- investigate topics of interest
- seek answers to research questions
- receive help on homework questions
- establish friendships with students around the world

## KidsCom
http://kidscom.com/

*KidsCom* has kids games, chat rooms for kids, video game cheats, and other activities for kids. The games focus on fun, learning, and Internet safety. There is also a link to *ParentsTalk*, a parenting magazine with parenting tips, family activities, crafts for children, help with a difficult child, and other parenting information.

## Homework Help
http://www.startribune.com/homework_help/

This web site serves as a homework resource for elementary, middle, or high school students. Students can get the help they need on their homework by posting questions to *The Minneapolis-St. Paul Star Tribune Homework Help* site. Questions are answered by volunteers who are 18 and over, from around the country.

*Why are email, listservs, and bulletin boards useful communication tools?*

Email is like leaving voice mail on someone's computer. It provides a fast, convenient method of communicating across distances. One of the chief benefits is the flexibility offered to senders and receivers of messages. As with voice mail, the receiver need not be present. The added advantage to email is that your message will be delivered even if the phone line is busy.

Mailing lists and bulletin boards simplify communication between individuals and groups. Whether connecting a teacher to a group of students or to a group of professionals sharing similar interests, mailing lists and bulletin boards provide multiple channels of communication in one convenient format.

## What is Telementoring?

Through the Internet you can tap into a whole new community of learners. Visiting someone's web site may introduce you to many new ideas. Yet this experience represents only one way of learning from the Internet. Exchanging ideas and information is another, more active way to learn from the Internet and World Wide Web.

Traditional mentoring involves an exchange between an expert and a novice. The expert/mentor is an experienced individual who gives guidance, support, and encouragement to the novice. Telementoring offers all the benefits of traditional mentoring by connecting experts and novices via email or the World Wide Web. The purpose of the mentoring might be to provide information on specific subjects or to provide guidance on life goals and decisions. Knowledgeable adults consult with students about their schoolwork, offering advice and critical feedback. Specific formats include:

- one to one
- moderated group

- unmoderated group
- peer mentoring

Telementoring provides opportunities for formal and informal communication between students, teachers, and professionals in the outside world. Multiple mentoring experiences are available:

- parent—student
- inservice teacher—preservice teacher
- content expert—student
- college student—high school student
- teacher—teacher

*How can I find out more about how telementoring works?*

One way to experience telementoring is by visiting a web site that simulates the actual telementoring process. You can choose to either follow the progress of one student's telementoring experience or participate in the experience yourself. Visit these sites to find out more about mentoring via the Internet.

**National School Network—Telementoring and Mentor Center**
http://nsn.bbn.com/telementor_wrkshp/tmlink.html

This web site includes numerous links to telementoring resources and articles, including *About Telementoring, How-To Guidelines,* and *Projects.*

**Telementoring Web: Adult Experts Assisting in the Classroom**
http://www.tnellen.com/cybereng/mentor/

This site offers an introduction to the concept of telementoring, including pros and cons, examples, and guidelines. Successful telementoring programs and a *Find a Telementor* link are also provided.

## How Can I Use Telementoring for Professional and Instructional Purposes?

Telementoring offers unique opportunities for both teachers and students. Teachers can either serve as a mentor for other individuals or link with a mentor of their own. Students can connect with mentors to receive individual assistance and personalized feedback.

The following are examples of how teachers can advance professional and instructional knowledge through telementoring:

- serve as a mentor to a student
- sign up as a mentor to a new teacher
- connect with a mentor regarding educational technology
- link with a mentor in a specific curricular area
- locate a mentor to help plan a new unit of study

Students can expand their knowledge and skills through telementoring by:

- receiving individual help on written assignments
- connecting with a mentor in a special area of interest
- getting feedback on homework
- linking with a mentor for research

Telementoring offers many advantages for teachers and students. Partnerships can be established to guide or reinforce learning. All participants can benefit from this unique experience.

***What are some suggested telementoring sites for professional and instructional use?***

### Electronic Emissary
http://emissary.ots.utexas.edu/emissary/index.html

This web site will help link volunteer professionals with teachers and their classrooms. You can apply to be involved in a new telementoring project, search a database of successful curriculum-based telementoring projects, or sign up as a subject matter expert.

### Tutor 2000
http://www.tutor2000.com/

*Tutor 2000* is the first nationwide online tutoring referral service. Professional and skilled tutors offer one-on-one academic assistance and skills development matched to the needs of the learner. Students and tutors meet in a chat room for private sessions.

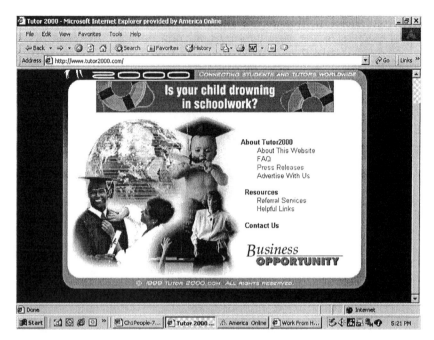

**International Telementor Program**
http://www.telementor.org/

Visit this site to learn about the International Telementor Program and how you can sign up to become a mentor. This site also has links to telementoring articles, research, and projects. The *Current News* section features a successful telementoring experience.

**AT&T Learning Network—Ask LN**
http://www.att.com/learningnetwork/whatln.html

Have a question about how to use technology in your classroom? This web site offers guidance and advice on educational technology issues. A network of mentors, teachers with experience integrating technology into the K-12 classroom, provide coaching and information on how to use technology effectively.

## What is "Ask an Expert"?

Teachers and students often have questions for which answers may not be easily found in a textbook. The World Wide Web offers one means for expanding your search. Several web sites provide access to an array of qualified "experts" who can help answer your questions. These experts might be teachers or professionals in the area you are researching. You can post your question to the expert by email or by visiting the appropriate web site. Answers are usually received in a few days or less.

### How Can I Use "Ask an Expert" for Professional and Instructional Purposes?

Teachers and students can benefit from "ask an expert" web sites.

Teachers can use "ask an expert" to:
- find answers to curricular-specific questions
- acquire professional resources
- discover curricular connections
- investigate professional development opportunities

Students can use "ask an expert" to:
- extend research projects
- find homework help
- investigate past discoveries
- separate fact from fiction

Visit some of the following "ask an expert" sites:

**The Savvy Cyber Teacher**
http://k12science.ati.stevens-tech.edu/cyberteacher/week2web.html

This site includes a variety of tips for using the Internet effectively in the K-12 classroom. An index of links, called "finding online experts," connects you with several "ask an expert" web pages, including sample projects that use online experts.

### NASA's Quest Project
http://quest.nasa.gov/index.html

This web site connects you to NASA's space scientists and space team and provides a directory of online events and interactive projects. This is a great resource for aspiring future astronauts.

### Ask Jeeves for Kids
http://www.ajkids.com/

Have a question about any topic? This simple question and answer format serves as a great resource for students and teachers.

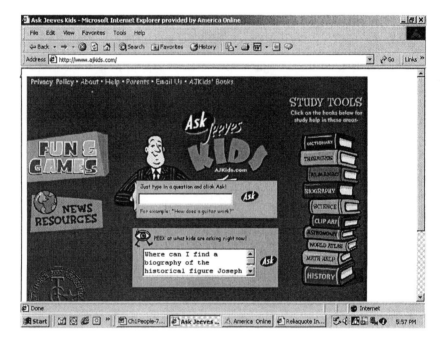

Used by permission of Ask Jeeves, Inc., Emeryville, CA, USA, copyright Ask Jeeves, Inc. 1996-2002, all rights reserved. The name "Ask Jeeves for Kids" is a trademark of Ask Jeeves, Inc.

**Access Excellence Resource Center**
http://www.accessexcellence.org/RC/askanexpert.html

The site provides links to a variety of "ask an expert" and homework help web sites, including *Ask Discover* and *Ask a Scientist.*

**About.**
http://inventors.about.com/cs/askanexpert/

This web site includes multiple links to "ask an expert" web sites, including *Ask an Expert—Factoids* and *Ask an Expert—How Stuff Works.*

*Summary*

This section introduced a variety of ways to communicate across the Internet, including three common forms: *email, listservs,* and *bulletin boards.* Several new forms of virtual communication were also presented, including *collaborative workspaces* and *web-based video conferencing. Telementoring* and *ask an expert* were introduced as additional resources for establishing communication across the Web.

In using the communication channels that the Web provides, teachers and students can benefit greatly by connecting to a vast number of people around the world. Communication and research skills can be enhanced, resulting in rich learning experiences for all involved. The classroom curriculum can be transformed as teaching and learning experiences extend beyond the existing school structure.

# CHAPTER 3
## ACCESS TO RESOURCES

The Web is a wonderful educational resource. Both teachers and students can use the Web to search for information on a variety of topics. A teacher can access thousands of lesson plans, categorized by grade level or subject matter. A student can access books in a library that is halfway around the world. In addition, there are numerous sites dedicated to educational research and funding opportunities. Finally, the Web provides teachers with an effective resource for professional development. In this section we discuss eight main uses of the Web:

- information source
- lesson plan bank
- image warehouse
- research tool
- learning tool
- evaluation tool
- professional development tool
- publishing tool

## How Can I Use the Web as an Information Source?

*ISTE NETS II: Teachers plan and design effective learning environments and experiences supported by technology.*

The Web is one of the foremost sources of information in this century. Students and teachers can easily visit web sites that contain information on a wide variety of topics.

Web documents, graphics, and audio and video clips all contribute to the learning experience. With a point and a click, students have access to government sites, museums, and libraries. Teachers have access to these resources as well as lesson plans and tutorials for professional development.

# What Are Search Engines?

The most efficient way to find information on the Web is to use a search engine. Search engines are programs that categorize information in databases and then retrieve that information in the form of searches. Search engines provide two levels of search options. First, most search engines categorize information into a table of contents. The user can look for information by clicking the links within the search engine's categorized index.

Search engines also use electronic robots, together with indexing software, to look through new web pages, searching for keywords within those pages. The keywords are stored in a database of information. This allows you to utilize another type of search by entering keywords associated with the topic on which you want information. The search engine database compares your search statement to the information in its database. It then returns a list of web pages that contain the keywords that you have entered.

For example, a search for the words "lesson plans" would return a number of different web sites that contain the words "lesson plans" somewhere on the page. The user would then visit one of the web sites listed by clicking on the link.

## How Can I Conduct an Effective Search?

Search engines use Boolean logic to compare keywords. Boolean logic can help limit your search through the use of AND, OR, and NOT in your keyword statement. As an example, a user can search for math AND elementary or math NOT secondary. A few tips for conducting an effective search include:

- The keywords that you use in your search should neither be too narrow nor too broad. For example, the word "education" is far too broad, but searching on the keywords "education AND fourth AND grade AND math NOT metrics" may be too narrow.
- If you get too many "hits" from a search, narrow it down using Boolean operators.
- Use the advanced search features that most engines have, such as limiting your search to web sites or images.

- Use more than one search engine to gather information; since each engine has its own database, results will differ.
- Use search engines that search more than one search engine at a time, thus saving you time.

There are many different search engines on the Web. Some of the more popular ones are:

**Google**
http://www.google.com

**Lycos**
http://www.lycos.com

**Ask Jeeves**
http://www.askjeeves.com

**Northern Light**
http://www.northernlight.com/

**Yahoo**
http://www.yahoo.com

**Alta Vista**
http://www.altavista.com/

**Infoseek**
http://infoseek.go.com

**Excite**
http://excite.com

Search engines designed specifically for students include:

**Yahooligans**
http://www.yahooligans.com

**Ask Jeeves for Kids**
http://www.ajkids.com

Search engines that explore multiple search engines simultaneously include:

**Profusion**
http://www.profusion.com

**SurfWax**
http://www.surfwax.com

**ixquick**
http://www.ixquick.com

**Dogpile**
http://www.dogpile.com/

One of the main reasons the Web has gained the attention of educational institutions is the availability of a wide variety of lesson plans and activities. Many teachers are creating web pages that describe successful plans or activities, often categorized by grade level or subject matter. Many web sites also include student and teacher ratings of lesson plans. Some web resources for locating lesson plans and curricular activities include:

**Columbia Education Center** (CEC)
http://www.col-ed.org/index.html

*CEC* contains over 600 lesson plans, all contributed by teachers. It also contains links to educational sites and resources, web guides, and web-based teaching resources.

**Education Resource List**
http://www.dpi.state.wi.us/dpi/dlcl/imt/ed_res.html

This listing includes over 400 sites divided into subject or curricular areas. General sites are listed first in each section, followed by sites related to specific subject areas or to K-12 education.

**California State University Northridge**
http://www.csun.edu/~hcedu013/plans.html

*California State University Northridge* links to hundreds of web sites categorized by grade level and subject matter. Many of the lesson plans contain corresponding teacher's guides.

**Collaborative Lesson Archive**
http://faldo.atmos.uiuc.edu/CLA/

The *Collaborative Lesson Archive (CLA)* is intended to be a forum for the creation, distribution, and archival of education curricula for all grade levels and subject areas. *CLA* provides the framework and the storage area; the quantity and quality of the content is entirely dependent on the Internet community.

34

## Education World
http://www.education-world.com

*Education World* is designed to help educators with lesson plans and classroom projects as well as in their own continuing educational and professional development. It features an education-specific search engine with links to over 100,000 sites. *Education World* offers monthly reviews of other educational web sites, grade-specific search engines, national education employment listings, curricular tools, lesson plans, forums, news, and other weekly original content.

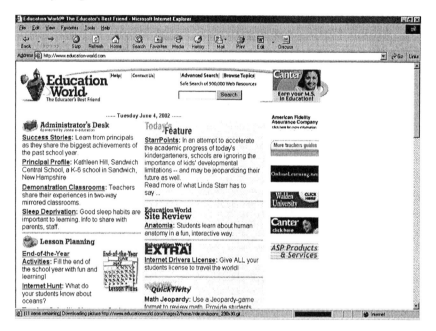

## New York Times Learning Network
http://www.nytimes.com/learning/

The *New York Times* web site is a storehouse of educational information. It contains current news articles rewritten for students

35

in grades 6-12. It is loaded with lesson plans, activities, crossword puzzles for kids, connections to this day in history, the latest educational news, and more.

### The Digital Classroom
http://www.nara.gov/education/teaching/teaching.html

This web site contains reproducible primary documents, lesson plans correlated to the national history standards, and cross-curricular connections.

### AskERIC Lesson Plan Collection
http://ericir.syr.edu/Virtual/Lessons/

The *AskERIC Lesson Plan Collection* contains more than 2,000 unique lesson plans that have been written and submitted by teachers from all over the United States.

### Apple Computers
http://henson.austin.apple.com/edres/lessonmenu.shtml

The *Apple Computers* site contains lesson plans by teachers for teachers, divided into elementary, middle, and high school levels.

## How Can I Use the Web as an Image Warehouse?

Communication is generally enhanced when pictures or graphics accompany the message. A web page message is often clearer and more interesting with the use of graphical images. Images also can help improve student projects and assignments. The Web is a storehouse of free images, but before using any images from the Web, check with the owners for copyright information and permission to use them. Some free resources include:

### Freeimages.com
http://www.freeimages.com

This web site includes photos, backgrounds, images, and animations, as well as free membership to other image banks.

**The Clip Art Gallery**
http://school.discovery.com/clipart/index.html

At this gallery, you can choose from hundreds of original clip art, including all types of graphical images and animations.

**Indexes of Education Images**
http://lunar.arc.nasa.gov/education/images/
http://www.blantonmuseum.org/education/images/

These web sites contain dozens of images for educational purposes. The interface lists the images, which can be displayed by simply clicking on the image name.

**Lycos Photo Center**
http://www.lycos.com/Photocenter

You can upload your favorite photos from this web site. In addition, the site includes tips and tricks to improve your photos.

## How Can I Use the Web as a Research Tool?

Initially, the primary users of the Internet were researchers at universities and governmental organizations. In the early 1990s, businesses realized that the Internet was a valuable tool for advertising their unique products or services and keeping track of the competition. Today, educational institutions are one of the fastest growing groups accessing information on the Internet.

There are many ways to use the Internet for research, including:

- exploring libraries to search for information
- locating articles and other documents related to your research topic
- visiting web sites directly related to your topic (e.g., animals, science)

Sites dedicated to educational research on the Web include:

**United States Department of Education**
http://www.ed.gov

The *U.S. Department of Education* includes links to the latest educational headlines, funding opportunities, student financial assistance, research and statistics, news and events, as well as a directory to other educational resources.

**Library Catalogs**
http://catalog.lib.ncsu.edu

This site provides a list of library catalogs, university libraries, and U.S. government libraries. Library servers on the World Wide Web (from the Berkeley Digital Library Sunsite) and library catalogs on the World Wide Web (from University of Saskatchewan Libraries) are also available.

**American Library Association**
http://www.ala.org

The *American Library Association* provides leadership for the development, promotion, and improvement of library and information services, and the profession of librarianship, to enhance learning and ensure access to information for all.

**Library of Congress**
http://www.loc.gov

The mission of the *Library of Congress* is to make its resources available to Congress and the American people. The *Library of Congress* attempts to preserve a collection of knowledge and creativity for future generations. Access to the *Library of Congress* also includes links to services for researchers and K-12 educators.

**The Internet Public Library**
http://ipl.sils.umich.edu

The *Internet Public Library (IPL)* was the first public library of the Internet. This site is committed to providing library services to the Internet community, to teaching what librarians have to contribute in a digital environment, to promoting librarianship and the importance of libraries, and to sharing interesting ideas and techniques with other librarians.

**Peterson's Education Center**
http://www.petersons.com/ugrad

This web site brings together, at one central address, consistently organized information about educational opportunities at all levels, and gives individuals the ability to search Peterson's databases. In addition, users can request more information and interact with faculty and administrators at educational institutions.

**American Educational Research Association (AERA)**
http://www.aera.net/pubs/rer

AERA is an international professional organization that encourages scholarly activity related to educational research. Its goal is to promote the application and dissemination of educational research. *AERA* includes links to educational journals.

**Educational Research Service (ERS)**
http://www.ers.org/

ERS is an independent organization designed to provide reliable, unbiased information to local school districts. It provides publications, periodicals, as well as custom information responses.

## How Can I Use the Web as a Learning Tool?

New web sites are being published every month at staggering rates. Teachers can use many of these sites to learn web basics, as well as techniques and tips for effective use of the Web in their classrooms. Some web resources that can be used as learning tools include:

**Internet 101**
http://www.internet101.org

This is a wonderful web site that provides information about Internet basics. It provides tips for getting started and safe surfing. It also has links to numerous web resources.

**CEARCH: The Cisco Educational Archive**
http://sunsite.unc.edu:80/cisco/web-arch.html

*CEARCH* is a resource for teachers and schools interested in finding out more about the Internet. The site provides information on how to use the Internet in the classroom, and how a school can get wired.

**Teacher/Pathfinder**
http://teacherpathfinder.org/

This educational Internet village provides access to a support office, schoolhouse, and professional development tools. The *Teacher's Village* link contains hot topics, field trips, and remediation information.

**Quest: NASA K-12 Internet Initiative**
http://quest.arc.nasa.gov

The mission of *Quest: NASA K-12 Internet Initiative* is to provide support and services for schools, teachers, and students to fully utilize the Internet and its underlying information technologies. Information is available on how to bring the Internet into your classroom, with a comprehensive look at Internet science.

**c/net**
http://www.cnet.com/

Learn about computer hardware, software, and gadgets at *c/net*. The latest technology is discussed at a level that is understandable. Web authoring topics also are discussed. This web site also provides access to downloads of new technology software.

**Digital Divide Network** (DDN)
http://www.digitaldividenetwork.org/content/sections/index.cfm

*DDN* provides educators with information on how to effectively utilize the Internet in the classroom. There are sections on access issues, literacy and learning, and current research funding.

# How Can I Use the Web as an Evaluation Tool?

*ISTE NETS IV: Teachers apply technology to facilitate a variety of effective assessment and evaluation strategies.*

Student assessment is an integral part of the educational process. It is important for teachers to know how well or how little a student understands the material delivered. The Web is a great source of information on many types of assessment techniques. The Web can help with assessment in three ways: it provides information about assessment; it provides actual tools (such as rubrics); and it provides a mechanism for storing and accessing electronic portfolios. The next three sections discuss web sites where you can find general information about assessment, rubrics, and portfolios.

## How Can I Use the Web to Find Information on Assessment?

Assessment is one of the most important components of education. Teachers need to assess their students' performance in order to determine if learning has occurred. Teachers also use assessment techniques to determine if the instruction itself is effective.

The Web contains many sites that discuss assessment concepts and techniques. The following sites can be used to find a plethora of information about assessment.

**Teaching Effectiveness Program—University of Oregon**
http://www.uoregon.edu/~tep/assessment/index.html

Classroom assessment techniques, team learning, and creating successful group assignments are all discussed at this site. In addition, the site addresses the topic of writing multiple-choice questions that demand critical-thinking skills.

**Assessment Topics**
http://www.leeds.ac.uk/sddu/assess/indtopic.htm

Links from this web site include assessment of creative work, project work, and student group activities. Guidance is provided on learning journals and self-assessment statements.

**Innovative Teaching Newsletter**
http://surfaquarium.com/newsletter/assessment.htm

This web site describes how assessment can provide feedback regarding the effectiveness of the instruction. Sample assessment techniques and links to multiple assessment topics are included.

**ETE Teacher Pages**
http://www.cotf.edu/ete/teacher/assessment.html

Good assessment should include what the student can do as well as what they should know. This web site contains an assortment of ideas and references on the art of assessment.

**Innovative Assessment**
http://www.lgu.ac.uk/deliberations/assessment/mowl_fr.html

This web site addresses the underlying philosophy and application of assessment techniques and tools. It discusses the benefits of utilizing more innovative approaches to assessment, rather than relying on the traditional forms of assessment utilized in most educational situations.

**AAHE Bulletin—Fair Assessment Practices**
http://www.aahe.org/bulletin/may2.htm

This bulletin addresses the importance of assessing your students fairly. It lists seven steps to fair assessment including having clearly stated learning outcomes, matching your assessment to what you teach, and using many different techniques. The site also has many valuable links to assessment policies and references.

**Assessing Your Students**
http://www.catl.uwa.edu.au/resources/assessment.pdf

This URL is a link to a downloadable document that discusses assessment. The booklet contains information about formative and summative assessment, as well as web-based assessment.

## How Can I Use the Web to Find Information on Rubrics?

A rubric is a printed set of scoring criteria that helps a teacher evaluate students' work. Rubrics are used to provide feedback to students on their level of learning for the specific instruction. Assessment criteria are clear and straightforward, which is beneficial for the teacher as well as the students.

The following sites provide information on creating and using rubrics in your classroom. Some sites even provide a mechanism for determining the effectiveness of the rubrics that you use.

**Rubrics for Web Lessons**
http://webquest.sdsu.edu/

Rubrics are particularly useful for assessing complex and subjective products (such as creative writing, art work, and technology products). This site lists resources for authentic assessment, sample rubrics, and guidelines for creating your own rubrics.

**Rubrics.com**
http://www.rubrics.com/

This web site discusses best practices of rubric design and makes suggestions for constructing criteria statements as well as examples of how to build rubrics.

**Kathy Schrock's Guide for Educators**
http://school.discovery.com/schrockguide/assess.html

Many links to subject-specific web pages and general rubrics are given on this web site. In addition, the site contains links to related rubric articles.

**Rubrics and Evaluation Resources**
http://www.ncsu.edu/midlink/ho.html

This site provides a generic rubric template and a multimedia template. The "how-to" link discusses why rubrics should be used and describes a process for constructing effective rubrics.

**Rubric, Rubrics, Teacher Rubric Makers**
http://teachers.teach-nology.com/web_tools/rubrics/

Rubric generators are provided on this web site. The options include basic reading skill, class participation, handwriting, research report, presentation, and listening rubric generators.

**RubiStar**
http://rubistar.4teachers.org/

You can use this web site to create rubrics for your project-based learning activities. A RubiStar is a tool to help teachers who want to use rubrics, but do not have time to create them from scratch. Another benefit of this site is that it provides a way for teachers to analyze the performance of the whole class.

## How Can I Use the Web to Find Information on Student Portfolios?

Portfolios are used in education to gather typical or exemplary samples of performance. In general, the purpose of a portfolio is to collect and present a compilation of materials that has been produced by students. Portfolio utilization is an ongoing process for monitoring student progress toward achieving stated performance outcomes.

**Notes from Research—Portfolio Assessment**
http://www.sdcoe.k12.ca.us/notes/5/portfolio.html

Assessment theory is discussed on this web site. In addition, a comprehensive look at assessment research can be found. The site also lists numerous portfolio success stories.

**Merrill Methods Cluster**
http://cwx.prenhall.com/bookbind/pubbooks/methods-cluster/chapter16/deluxe.html

This web site links you to numerous assessment resources. It discusses electronic portfolios for both students and teachers.

**Electronic Portfolios**
http://electronicportfolios.com/portfolios.html

Technology can be used to support electronic portfolios. This web site contains references and links, online publications, conference presentations, and workshop training sessions.

**CRESST**
http://www.cse.ucla.edu/CRESST/Reports/TECH371.PDF

This report from the National Center for Research on Evaluation, Standards, and Student Testing (CRESST) discusses whether portfolios can assess student performance and influence instruction. The report is a downloadable 165 pages of thought-provoking information.

**The Electronic Learning Community**
http://www.pgcps.org/~elc/portfolio.html

This web site describes what a portfolio is and why teachers would want to use this assessment technique. It contains links to characteristics of effective portfolios, the phases of portfolio development, and ideas on how to start using portfolios.

## How Can I Use the Web for Professional Development?

*ISTE NETS V: Teachers use technology to enhance their productivity and professional practice.*

Professional development has never been easier than it is on the Internet. Tutorials, online forums and courses, and pages of text resources are available to help educators learn more about technology and its use in the classroom. Distance education is becoming more of a reality because of the supporting technologies and the proliferation of information. Some professional development web sites include:

**Web Teacher**
http://www.webteacher.org/macnet/indextc.html

A web tutorial is available at this web site. It includes information about how to communicate using the Web (email, newsgroups, mail lists), using multimedia (working with images, sounds, movies), and home page construction.

**Tapped In**
http://www.tappedin.org

*Tapped In* is an online community of education professionals, including teachers and librarians. You can find links to special resources that give examples of online activities.

**CARET**
http://caret.iste.org/

The *Center for Applied Research in Educational Technology* (CARET) is a project of the International Society for Technology in Education. It provides an extensive question and answer section with links to student learning, curriculum and instruction, and professional development. The site includes a very easy-to-use search utility from which you can find numerous research studies on a variety of topics. Links to helpful web sites for educators are also available.

**The Virtual Schoolhouse Career Development**
http://metalab.unc.edu/cisco/schoolhouse/lounge/career.html

The *Virtual Schoolhouse Career Development* web site contains links to professional development sites. Links include sites at which you can take courses via the Internet, find out about educational conferences, and read the latest publications.

### Educational Technology Training Center (ETTC) for Middlesex County, NJ
http://www.techtrain.org/

*ETTC* is a comprehensive resource for educators in Middlesex County, New Jersey and throughout the world. The site includes technology integration workshops, lesson plans, links to Internet resources, tips on teaching in a one-computer classroom, and more.

### Apple Education—Staff Development
http://www.apple.com/education/professionaldevelopment/

Simply putting computers in classrooms does not guarantee a positive change in teaching and learning. The success of technology in schools depends on the skills of the teacher. This site provides a staff development forum that helps teachers learn to use technology tools with the same ease they use books, maps, pencils, and pens. The *Apple Virtual Campus* (http://www.apple.com/education/k12/events/semseries/) contains a series of virtual seminars that show how schools successfully choose digital content and how they integrate technology into the curriculum.

### From Now On: The Educational Technology Journal
http://fromnowon.org/

This web site provides a variety of professional development tools. Articles on many educational topics are available, including those on Internet policies, staff development, research, and parenting.

### Engines for Education
http://www.ils.nwu.edu/~e_for_e/nodes/I-M-INTRO-ZOOMER-pg.html

This web site has a series of questions and answers to some of the most important educational issues today.

### *Summary*

The teaching and learning opportunities on the Internet are endless. Teachers, students, administrators, and parents can all find valuable information and resources by conducting effective searches. Educational institutions are just beginning to scratch the surface of the Internet. The future promises to hold many more opportunities.

## How Do I Use the Web as a Publishing Tool?

*ISTE NETS I: Teachers demonstrate a sound understanding of technology operations and concepts.*

So far in this book, we have focused on *getting* information from the Internet. The Internet would not be what it is today, however, without people *putting* information on the Internet. There are numerous web sites with information on setting up web sites in your school and publishing your own web pages. What better resource could there be *about* the Web than one that you find *on* the Web?

Like print media, web pages have one main purpose: to convey information. In an educational setting, a web page can be used:

- to convey background information about the school
- as a notification board for parents regarding meeting times, important dates, days off, lunch menu
- to display curriculum, lesson plans, teachers' biographies
- to publish student work

### What are web pages, web sites, and web servers?

There are many terms that are important to understand before discussing web page development.

- A *web page* is a document that you view in your browser (e.g., Internet Explorer, Netscape). The document can fill one screen or multiple screens, giving the user the ability to scroll down to view it all.
- A *web site* is a group of web pages that are created and maintained by a group or individual.
- A *web server* is a computer that runs software that allows web pages to be "served" or shown via a browser. The

information stored on a web server is available to anyone with access to the Internet.

- A web page is *published* (or uploaded to a web server) by using the publishing feature provided in the authoring tools or by using File Transfer Protocol (FTP) software.

## What Tools Do You Need to Create a Web Page?

Creating a web page can be a valuable and fun exercise for both teachers and students. Many school systems have extensive web sites that list valuable information about their use of technology.

There are two main ways to create your own web page:

- use a web authoring tool
- use a programming language

These techniques are discussed in the following sections.

### What are Web Authoring Tools?

Using a web authoring tool is a great idea for those who do not want to become programmers. Web authoring tools are sophisticated software packages that provide an easy way to create web pages. Templates and themes are available in most of these products that allow the user to create entire web sites. The following web authoring programs are easy to use and provide a number of powerful and useful functions. Most products can be downloaded from the URL listed, for a 30-day free trial.

**Microsoft FrontPage**
http://www.microsoft.com

**Adobe Systems PageMill**
http://www.adobe.com

**Web Wizard**
http://www.halcyon.com/artamedia/webwizard

**DreamWeaver**
http://www.macromedia.com/software/dreamweaver

**NetObjects Fusion**
http://www.netobjects.com

*How Can I Use Hypertext Markup Language (HTML)?*

Hypertext Markup Language (HTML) is the simplest, most commonly used programming language of the Web. HTML has become a popular choice for web development because it is platform-independent, allowing web pages to be viewed on any type of computer (Mac or PC).

A set of special instructions, called HTML tags, is used to mark, or specify the format of, the text that is to be displayed on the web page. Most, but not all, HTML tags come in pairs, with a *begin text* format <begin> and an *end text* format </end> tag required.

Numerous web sites contain information on HTML programming. Some of these are listed below.

**Setting up a Web Site for Your School: An Online Presentation**
http://www.fred.net/nhhs/html2/present.htm

This guide is a starting point for school web site generation and management. Visitors can download or distribute the documents found at this site as long as credit is given to the author and the web site of North Hagerstown High School.

**How Do They Do That with HTML?**
http://www.nashville.net/~carl/htmlguide

Though content is truly the most important part of any web page, aesthetics of the page are also important. Suggestions on this site may help with the aesthetics.

**HTML Crash Course for Educators**
http://edweb.cnidr.org/htmlintro.html

This tutorial will introduce you to the basics of HTML design and style. The *Crash Course* was designed with teachers in mind.

**CERN—Web Authoring**
http://webservices.web.cern.ch/WebServices/AuthoringDoc/Authorin
g.htm

*CERN* contains web authoring tutorials and links to many web
authoring sites. A non-exhaustive list of tools to use is categorized
by platform. A series of HTML tutorials are available in
collaboration with the IT/User support group.

**Classroom Internet Server Cookbook**
http://web66.coled.umn.edu/Cookbook/Default.html

This is a cookbook that gives recipes for setting up an Internet
server in a classroom. Each recipe includes links so that you can
download every ingredient that you need.

*What Does a Sample Web Page Look Like in HTML?*

HTML code can be created by using a simple text editor, such as
SimpleText on a Mac, or Notepad on Windows. Word processing
software also can be used to write HTML code. If you use an
authoring tool to develop your web pages, the tool itself creates the
HTML for the page. There are three basic steps to creating a web
page:

1. Start your text editor and type in the HTML tags and text.
2. Save the file with a .htm or .html extension.
3. View the HTML file in a web browser.

There are a few HTML tags that make up a basic web page, as listed
below:

```
<HTML>
<HEAD>
<TITLE>
```
This is where a brief description of the purpose of the web page is
inserted. The text between the title tags displays on the title bar of
the browser, rather than the web page contents area.
```
</TITLE>
</HEAD>
<BODY>
```

This is where the content of the web page is inserted. This text displays in the content area of the browser.
</BODY>
</HTML>

If you see something on a web page that you would like to incorporate into your own web page, you can see how the page was created by viewing the source code of the page. You can do this by selecting View from the menu bar and then selecting Source. Sites listed previously contain more HTML tags and their uses.

## How Can I Create My Own Web Pages?

Let's create a very simple web page using word processing software. Microsoft Word has many new features that can help you make a web page with links, scrolling text, buttons, text boxes, sounds, and movies. You can also easily view the web page directly from Word, as it will display in the browser. Follow the three steps below to create a web page using Microsoft Word. The finished product is included for reference.

1. Using Microsoft Word, type in the following seven lines of information. Press the Enter key twice to create blank lines in between the text.

---

Interesting Places on the Web

Visit the Whitehouse
http://www.whitehouse.gov

Find information at the U.S. Department of Education
http://www.ed.gov

View a great glossary of Internet terms
http://www.matisse.net/files/glossary.html

---

(Notice that the URL text changes to blue, underlined text when you press the Enter key. Word automatically makes that text a link to the URL that you have entered.)

2. Use the standard Word formatting tools to format the first line of text as bold, font size 20, with a color of red. Highlight all other lines of text and format them as font size 14.

3. Save the file as a web page by clicking File on the menu bar of the text editor and then clicking Save as Web Page. The filename will automatically be saved with an extension of .htm or .html so that it can be viewed in a browser. For this sample, name the file "mypage.htm." You can view the HTML code by clicking View on the menu bar and then clicking HTML Source.

Now that the file is saved, it can be viewed in your browser by clicking File on the menu bar of the browser and then clicking Open. Type the filename that you gave when you saved the file (mypage.htm) into the address text box of the browser and press the Enter key. With the steps that you completed above, you created the web page shown below.

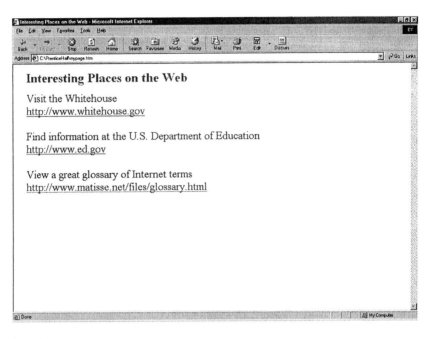

Sample page

## *Summary*

The World Wide Web is as extensive as it is today because of the web pages that have been published over the last 10 years. Educators are getting more involved with the Web today by creating web pages for themselves, their classes, or together with their students. Many of the most popular and interesting web sites are those that have been created by individual classes or teachers. Contributing information to the Web is becoming an important role for everyone in the field of education.

# CHAPTER 4
# ACCESS TO CURRICULAR CONNECTIONS

*ISTE NETS III: Teachers implement curriculum plans that include methods and strategies for applying technology to maximize student learning.*

The Internet offers an incredible array of resources for teachers who wish to transform their curricula by incorporating the sights, sounds, and experiences offered through the Web. For example, the Internet allows students to:

- interact with people from other countries and cultures
- compile an investment portfolio
- take a tour of the circulatory system
- dissect a frog
- interact with NASA scientists
- access real data (e.g., census, weather, investments)
- participate, virtually, in critical historical events
- develop research and writing skills
- publish literary and art work

Of course, these examples barely scratch the surface of the possibilities available on the Web. Students can visit other countries, converse with famous authors and scientists, take virtual tours of famous art and historical museums, interact with other students, and even get help with their homework. The problem is there are so many sites available that it is hard to know where to begin.

Generally, when teachers first start using the Internet as a curricular resource, they tend to work within established content areas. For that reason, this chapter is organized around common school subjects. Within each content area, we point you to some of the best web sites available. In addition, most of these sites lead to other sites with related information.

The Web offers many opportunities for students to explore the mathematical concepts involved in everyday situations. The sites listed here are aimed at primary, secondary, and post-secondary students. In addition, we include sites that teachers will find useful for professional development.

**National Council of Teachers of Mathematics (NCTM)**
http://www.nctm.org/about/

NCTM is the largest nonprofit professional association of mathematics educators dedicated to improving the teaching and learning of mathematics. NCTM offers vision, leadership, and communication avenues for mathematics educators at all levels. Their site provides information about mathematics standards, related conferences, as well as links to lesson plans, activities, and projects.

**International Journal for Mathematics Teaching and Learning**
http://www.ex.ac.uk/cimt/ijmtl/ijmenu.htm

This journal, published only in electronic form, is aimed at practitioners who are interested in enhancing mathematics teaching for all ages and abilities up to 18 years. The journal provides a medium for stimulating and challenging ideas, offering innovation and practice in all aspects of mathematics teaching and learning.

**Ask Dr. Math**
http://mathforum.org/dr.math/index.html

Have a math question? If so, then check out *Ask Dr. Math.* This site is a question and answer service for K-12 students and their teachers. Users can search an archive by level and topic, as well as a section devoted to Frequently Asked Questions (FAQs).

**Mega Mathematics**
http://www.cs.uidaho.edu/~casey931/mega-math/

*MegaMath* makes challenging and interesting topics in math and computer science (algorithms, infinity, logic) accessible to elementary school kids. This site includes stories, games, and projects on a variety of math topics. By incorporating interactivity and exploiting the available technology, *MegaMath* creates interesting and fun math-based web materials.

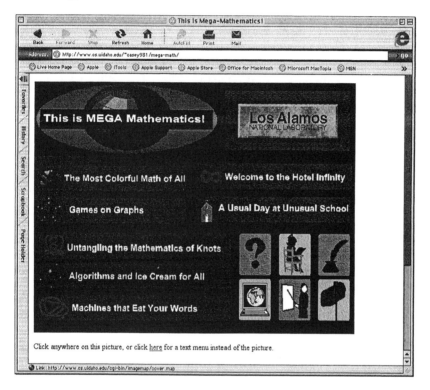

## MathMagic
http://forum.swarthmore.edu/mathmagic/

*MathMagic* is a K-12 telecommunications project hosted by the Math Forum. It combines students' uses of computers with the development of problem-solving strategies and communications skills. *MathMagic* posts challenges in each of four grade categories (K-3, 4-6, 7-9, and 10-12) and encourages each registered team to pair up with another registered team to engage in a problem-solving dialogue.

## Young Investor
http://www.younginvestor.com/flash/index_flash.html

The *Young Investor* web site is an excellent way for teens to learn the fundamentals of money and investing in a comfortable, familiar, and interactive environment. This site includes information about how to save money or start a business and also includes a question and answer section for parents. Try out the college calculator or see how well you fare playing a simulated stock market game.

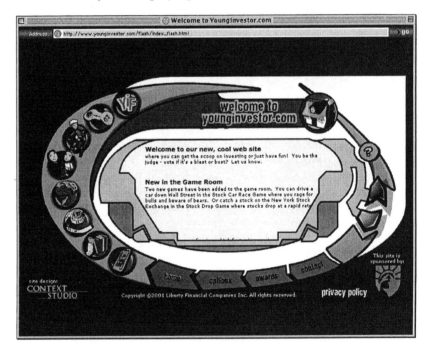

Copyright (2001-2002) Liberty Funds Distributor Inc., a member of Columbia Management Group. Reprinted with permission.

**Investing for Kids**
http://library.thinkquest.org/3096/

This site, designed by middle and high school students, includes activities for learners at all levels (elementary through college). *Investing for Kids* teaches the principles of saving and investing to both beginners and seasoned investors by helping students examine stocks, bonds, and mutual funds. An exciting feature of this site is the inclusion of a stock market game that helps users learn how to invest. In addition to reading about the concepts of investing, students can use the Java goal calculator, take a financial quiz, put together a stock portfolio, check out the stock learning center, look up terms in the glossary, and find out about collaborative projects.

**PlaneMath**
http://www.planemath.com

*PlaneMath* makes math educational materials readily accessible to students with disabilities, particularly physical disabilities. This site is designed specifically to stimulate and motivate special needs students in grades 4-7 to pursue aeronautics-related careers.

**AAA Math**
http://www.aaamath.com/index.html

This site contains hundreds of web pages of basic math skills for grades K-8. Each page includes an explanation of the math topic, opportunities for interactive practice, as well as several challenge games per topic.

**Math in Daily Life**
http://www.learner.org/exhibits/dailymath

This site explores how math helps us in our daily lives. By understanding the use of numbers in common situations, such as playing games or cooking, we learn to make important decisions. This site illustrates how math helps us shop wisely, buy the best insurance, remodel a home within a budget, understand population growth, or even bet on the horse with the best chance of winning a race.

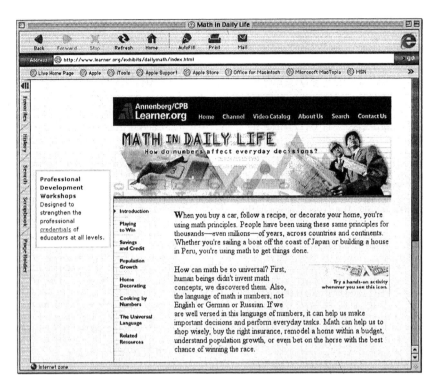

Copyright (1997-2002) Annenberg/CPB. Reprinted with permission.

### Project Interactivate
http://www.shodor.org/interactivate/

*Project Interactivate* provides interactive courseware for middle school mathematics explorations. "Interactivated" lessons, discussions, and activities enable teachers to extend hands-on activities and teach new content areas, incorporating technology appropriately. Materials are designed to be adapted easily to any standards-based, middle school mathematics text and include activities related to numbers and operations, functions and algebra, geometry and measurement, and data analysis and probability.

# How Can the World Wide Web Engage Students in Science?

The Internet provides tremendous opportunities for updating and enriching the traditional textbook-based science curriculum. For example, pictures from Mars, interviews with noted scientists, live experiments, and monitoring of weather changes are all readily available through the World Wide Web. In addition, massive amounts of real-time information are available.

## National Science Teachers Association (NSTA)
http://www.nsta.org

NSTA is the largest organization in the world committed to promoting excellence and innovation in science teaching and learning. To address subjects of critical interest to science educators, the Association publishes four journals and offers many links to other publications. NSTA conducts national and regional conventions that attract more than 30,000 attendees annually including science teachers, administrators, scientists, and business and industry representatives involved in science education.

## NASA's Educational Program
http://www.nasa.gov
http://www.hq.nasa.gov/office/codef/education/index.html

NASA collaborates with professional education associations, state and local education authorities, universities, private enterprise, and other organizations to develop instructional products that are consistent with the national curriculum standards and state or local curriculum frameworks. NASA's products are developed in multiple formats, with an emphasis on innovative applications of educational technology and interactive strategies.

## National Wildlife Federation (NWF)
http://www.nwf.org/

NWF focuses its efforts on environmental news and programs, and sites include a range of educational projects. For example, NWF's Environmental Education site (http://www.nwf.org/education/) offers both online and printed conservation education materials to elementary and middle school teachers and students who are learning about the environment and how to care for it.

NWF's Kids Zone site (http://www.nwf.org/kids/) is devoted to kids' activities and includes links to games, Ranger Rick, tours of amazing environments, and quizzes to see how much was learned.

## The National Space Science Data Center (NSSDC)
http://nssdc.gsfc.nasa.gov/

NSSDC provides access to a wide variety of astrophysics, space physics, solar physics, lunar, and planetary data from NASA space flight missions. Spacecraft and experiments that have or will provide public access data are also accessible through NSSDC. There are multiple links to photographic images, publications, and other outer space sites.

## One Sky, Many Voices
http://www.onesky.umich.edu/

This web site is dedicated to the creation of innovative, inquiry-based K-12 science curricula. CD-ROM and Internet-enhanced programs, focused on environmental science themes, are offered and include *Kids as Global Scientists*, *BioKIDS*, and *Hurricanes*.

## EnchantedLearning.com
http://www.enchantedlearning.com/Home.html

*EnchantedLearning* produces children's educational web sites and games to promote creativity and learning. This web site offers a variety of resources for classroom teachers, including animal print outs, world flags, books to make, anatomy, and nursery rhymes.

## Rader's Kapili.com
http://www.kapili.com/index.html

This is the home page of the 4kids.com series—chem4kids, biology4kids, geography4kids, and physics4kids. This site is full of information to help teach the sciences, including easy-to-read definitions, graphics, and activities about the atmosphere, atoms, motion, cells, earth's structure, vertebrates, light, and much more.

## VolcanoWorld
http://volcano.und.edu

*VolcanoWorld* is designed for anyone who has a special interest in volcanoes. The University of North Dakota first posted the site in 1995 and is celebrating seven successful years on the Internet. While visiting the site you can ask a vocanologist a question, view the most recent eruptions around the world, find out about volcano-related conferences, locate lesson plans, and even participate in volcano-related games.

## Solar System Simulator
http://space.jpl.nasa.gov/

The *Solar System Simulator* is a collaborative project of NASA, the Jet Propulsion Laboratory (JPL), and the California State Polytechnic University that offers a "spyglass on the cosmos." The web-based simulator can create a color image of any planet or satellite as seen from any point in the solar system.

## Beakman & Jax
http://www.beakman.com

*Beakman & Jax* is a newspaper comic strip by Jok R. Church. Using these characters as a central theme, this site offers science lesson activities. You can see your name written in hieroglyphics, tour the human body, or find answers to over 50 different questions such as "How do CDs work?" "Where do dreams come from?"

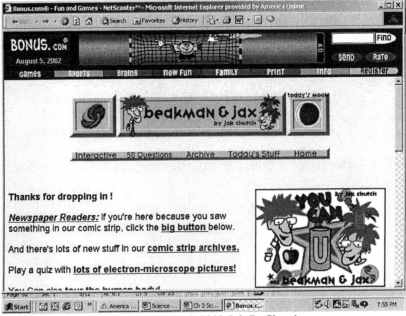

Presented by Bonus.com. Copyright © 2002 Jok R. Church—All Rights Reserved. Reprinted with permission.

**The Heart:  An Online Exploration**
http://sln2.fi.edu/biosci/heart.html

Designed for multiple grade levels, this web site allows learners to explore the wonders of the human heart.  Students can follow the blood through the vessels or wander through the web-like body systems.  They also can learn about how to have a healthy heart, how to monitor their heart's health, and listen to actual heartbeats.  Students can even watch a video of heart bypass surgery.

## How Can the World Wide Web Engage Students in the Social Sciences?

Technology offers teachers and students the opportunity to interact with social sciences content (e.g., history, social studies, geography, civics, and economics) in ways that build an increased understanding of world politics and geography. The Internet allows students to interact with voluminous amounts of timely information, as well as with students from classrooms around the world.

**Directory of Social Studies, Social Science, Art, & Music Education-Related Organizations**
http://www.indiana.edu/~ssdc/orgs.htm

This directory lists non-commercial organizations, including professional organizations concerned with the social studies, social sciences, art education, music education, or related topics.  Many of these organizations publish curriculum and teaching guides, lesson plans, journals, and magazines; conduct conventions, conferences, teacher workshops and seminars; and offer other types of services, support, and resources for educators.  This site includes links to the U.S. Department of Education, the National Council for the Social Studies, The National Library of Education, and the Ackerman Center for Democratic Education, located at Purdue University.

**Social Studies Resources for Educators**
http://falcon.jmu.edu/~ramseyil/social.htm

This site includes an extensive number of resources for educators in the social studies, including general links, reference materials, literature and lesson plans. Some of the links include the *Genealogy Home Page, This Day in History, Historical Fiction,* and a *Presidential Unit.*

## NationalGeographic.com
http://www.nationalgeographic.com/education/index.html

The *National Geographic* education home page includes links to lesson plans, online adventures, maps and geography, a teacher community, and a teacher store. Teachers will find photos, sounds, and printable maps on this web site. The online *World* magazine offers brainteaser games and other fun things for kids to try.

## GlobalSchoolNet—Field Trips
http://www.gsn.org/project/fieldtrips/

By visiting this web site you can join a field trip in another state or invite others to join your own field trip. This project encourages students to share their visits, observations, and discoveries with students and classes all over the world. In turn, you and your students can benefit from the excursion reports posted by other classes as you vicariously accompany these other classes on their field trips.

## History/Social Studies for K-12 Teachers
http://my.execpc.com/~dboals/boals.html

This web site offers a vast list of Internet resources for the K-12 history and social studies teacher. You will find information on museums around the world, government, geography, archeology, religion, European and American history, and much more.

**History/Social Studies For K-12 Teachers**

The major purpose of this home page is to encourage the use of the World Wide Web as a tool for learning and teaching and to provide some help for K-12 classroom teachers in locating and using the resources of the Internet in the classroom.

I know a What's New is overdue!

SELECT FROM THE MENU CHOICES BELOW

| |Archaeology| | |Creative Applications| | |Diversity| | |Electronic Texts, Books and Zines| |
| |Genealogy| | |General Guides| | |Geography/Economics| | |Government| |
| |General History| | |Non-Western History Sites| | |European/Russian History| | |American History| |
| |Humanities/Art| | |K-12 Resources| | |Kids and Students| | Colosseum/Flavian Amphitheatre |
| |Resources For Writers| | |Research/Critical Thinking| | |Media Sites/ Media Literacy| | |Religion/Ethics/ Philosophy| |
| |Resources For Parents| | |News/Current Events| | Seniors/Health | |
| Museo Archeologico Nazionale Napoli (Part 1) | Museo Archeologico Nazionale Napoli (Part 2) | Barcelona Archeological Museum (Part 1) | Barcelona Archeological Museum (Part 2) |
| Galleria dell' Accademy | Reserved for future files | Reserved for future files | Reserved for future files |

Teaching a class this Summer? Ask your students to suggest a caption for this photo and write a story for a prize.

Not copyrighted. Reprinted with permission.

## Awesome Library
http://www.awesomelibrary.org/social.html

This web site includes a number of links to resources, including lesson plans, current events, ecology, history, biographies, holidays, economics, and government. Teachers can search for lesson plans by grade level or theme. Additional lesson plans focused on multidisciplinary and multicultural activities are also provided.

## Social Science Data Collection (SSDC)
http://ssdc.ucsd.edu/index.html

*SSDC* is a collection of numeric data in the social sciences maintained by the Social Sciences and Humanities Library of University of California, San Diego. Students can engage in online data analysis and use spreadsheet applications to examine U.S.

budget information, population and housing data, and current demographic data.

**SCORE:  Schools of California Online Resources for Education**
http://score.rims.k12.ca.us/

This site includes history and social science resources, selected by a team of California educators, for their grade appropriateness, accuracy, and richness of content.  Links are included to grade-leveled lessons; curricula frameworks, content-based standards, and assessment measures; professional development resources, and virtual projects and field trips.

**Trib.com**
http://www.trib.com/NEWS/

*Trib.com* links to numerous news sources including *World News, U.S. News, Sports, Arts, Science, Business,* and the *AP Press.*

**How far is it?**
http://www.indo.com/distance/

This service uses data from the U.S. Census Bureau and a supplementary list of cities from around the world to find the latitude and longitude of two places, and then calculates the distance between them (as the crow flies). It also provides a map showing the two places, using the Xerox PARC Map.

**Explorer Trail: Multicultural Curriculum Resources**
http://ernie.wmht.org/trail/explor02.htm

This site features *Walk a Mile in My Shoes,* a year-long language curriculum that uses literature to teach children to know, understand, and respect others by recognizing the similarities among people while appreciating the differences.  Links are provided to resources that can enhance a multicultural curriculum.

## Kids Web Japan
http://jin.jcic.or.jp/kidsweb/

*Kids Web Japan* introduces students, ages 10-14, to the sights
and sounds of Japan. By visiting this site, you can find basic
information about Japan including regions of Japan, nature and
climate, daily life, schools, politics, and history.

## Smithsonian Institution National Museum of the American Indian
http://www.si.edu/nmai/

This site invites teachers and students to take a virtual field trip
to the *Smithsonian's National Museum of the American Indian,*
dedicated to the preservation, study, and exhibition of the life,
languages, literature, history, and arts of Native Americans.
The museum's collections span more than 10,000 years of
Native heritage.

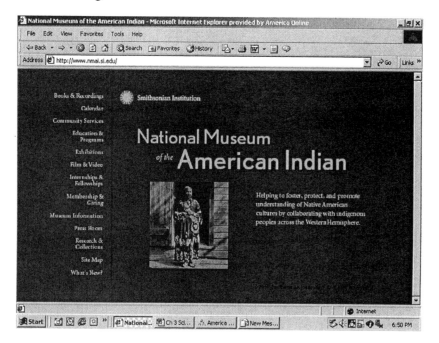

## How Can the World Wide Web Engage Students in Literacy and Language Arts?

The World Wide Web provides powerful support for developing reading and writing skills. Students seem particularly motivated to write well when they have an audience who will read their work. In addition, students can interact with both famous and obscure authors, access writing resources, and even play language games that sharpen important skills.

### National Council of Teachers of English
http://www.ncte.org

The National Council of Teachers of English is devoted to improving the teaching and learning of English and the language arts at all levels of education. Members are teachers and supervisors of English programs in elementary and secondary schools, faculty in college and university English departments, teacher educators, and local and state agency English specialists. This page leads to related sites including the national standards for English and a large collection of teaching ideas and materials.

### Kids' Web—A WWW Digital Library for Schoolkids
http://www.kidsvista.com/index.html

The goal of *Kids' Web* is to provide access to a subset of the Web that is simple to navigate. Each subject section contains a list of links to information that is understandable and interesting to kids. There are also links to external lists of material on each subject that more advanced students can browse for further information. If you take the *Arts* link to the *Literature* link you will find sections on *Children's Books* including online books, children's authors, fictional works, creative writing resources, as well as resources that allow you to explore the worlds of poetry and theater.

### The Children's Literature Web Guide
http://www.acs.ucalgary.ca/~dkbrown/index.html

The *Children's Literature Web Guide* gathers and categorizes the growing number of Internet resources related to books for children and young adults. The information on these pages is provided by fans, schools, libraries, and commercial businesses involved in the book world. Links to current book awards are also included.

## Lit Cafe
http://library.thinkquest.org/17500/

The *Lit Cafe* uses the metaphor of a coffee house to guide users through the basics of literature, within an intriguing and informative setting. This virtual classroom allows visitors to read biographies of famous authors or their works; play *CafeLibs,* a version of *MadLibs;* and submit original work to the bulletin board.

## Bartleby.com
http://www.bartleby.com/

This web site provides students, teachers, and researchers with unlimited access to books and information on the Web. You can find an encyclopedia, dictionary, thesaurus, and other reference books at *Bartleby.com.* There are daily and weekly updates on the home page as well as a featured author section.

## Project Gutenberg
http://www.promo.net/pg

*Project Gutenberg* provides access to full texts that no longer have a copyright (generally pre-1923). E-texts of Shakespeare, Poe, and Dante's works are included together with the books by Sir Arthur Conan Doyle and Lewis Carroll. Although some e-texts are still copyrighted, you can download them and read them for free.

## Laura Ingalls Wilder, Frontier Girl
http://webpages.marshall.edu/~irby1/laura.htmlx

This web site is devoted to the life and works of Laura Ingalls Wilder, American pioneer and children's author of the famous *Little House* books. Designed to provide information about Ms. Wilder and the places and characters mentioned in her books, this site is interactive, informational, and entertaining.

**Into the Wardrobe: The C. S. Lewis WWW Site (1898-1998)**
http://cslewis.DrZeus.net/

Developed by a fan of C. S. Lewis, this web site began as a short list of books written by Lewis and grew as a result of the contributions of others. The site includes links to a biography of Lewis, sound and photo links, message forums, chat rooms, related web sites, and personal anecdotes contributed by friends and relatives of Lewis.

**The Grammar Gorillas**
http://www.funbrain.com/grammar/

*Grammar Gorillas*, geared toward helping students identify parts of speech, is just one activity students will like at the *FunBrain* site (http://www.funbrain.com/index.html). Other language arts activities include creating word search puzzles, playing hangman, finding misspelled words, learning new words, and writing stories.

**Kid Crosswords and Other Puzzles**
http://www.kidcrosswords.com/

*Kid Crosswords and Other Puzzles* provides educators and parents with free puzzles that are designed to develop children's minds. Although "fun" puzzles are published, the primary goal is to provide creative and high-quality educational resources. Posted puzzles focus on a specific topic (civil rights, Africa, division). All kinds of puzzles are available: word search, rebus, crossword, scramble, connect-the-dots, and picture builders, to name a few.

**Online Writing Lab (OWL)**
http://owl.english.purdue.edu/

If you need help with your writing, Purdue University's *Online Writing Lab* is available 24 hours a day. *OWL* offers resources on writing skills, resources for students learning English as a second language, and resources on writing resumes. Over 125 handouts on writing skills are available to help students hone their skills. Teachers can also find links to writing-related resources, style guides, children's resources, and professional writing organizations.

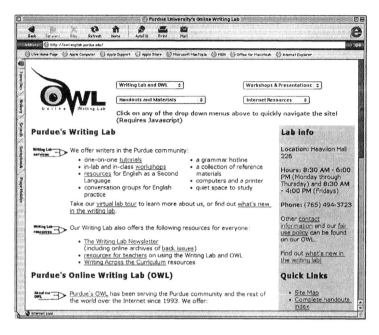

Copyright (1995-2002) by OWL at Purdue University. Reprinted with permission.

# How Can the World Wide Web Engage Students in Art, Music, and Physical Education?

Technology has always played a part in the arts by providing the tools, materials, and processes to facilitate artists' creative expression. Also, web sites related to physical education provide invaluable resources from which students, coaches, teachers, and parents will benefit.

## How Can I Use the Web to Find Information on Art Education?

Many web sites can be found that address the use of art in education. These sites provide resources such as lesson plans, art project ideas, as well as connections to other art teachers. The following web sites provide access to a few art education sites.

### Kids' Corner: Kids' Art
http://kids.ot.com/

This site is devoted to publishing kids' stories, poems, artwork, crafts, and photography. The site is intended primarily for children ages 1-16. New exhibits are published weekly.

### Make a Splash with Color
http://www.thetech.org/exhibits_events/online/color/intro/

This web site has three main sections: *Talking about Color, The Lighter Side of Color,* and *An Eye on Color.* Through a variety of activities and exhibits, students can explore different "ingredients of color," can observe the way color changes when it is reflected off objects or routed through tinted lenses, and can understand why our eyes sometimes see the "wrong" color.

### ArtsEdNet
http://www.getty.edu/artsednet/

*ArtsEdNet* is an online service developed by the Getty Education Institute for the Arts, to support the needs of the K-12 arts education community. It focuses on helping arts educators, general classroom teachers using the arts in their curricula, museum educators, and university faculty involved in the arts. *ArtsEdNet* disseminates information through the Internet and encourages the exchange of ideas and experiences regarding advocacy, and professional, curricular, and theory development.

### Arts: Blacksbury Electronic Village
http://www.bev.net/community/arts.html

This site includes multiple relevant links to online art exhibits, education in the arts, art organizations, as well as museums, theaters, galleries, and even nightclubs.

## How Can I Use the Web to Find Information on Music Education?

Many music education resources are available on the Web. Online games, chat rooms, and music encyclopedias are but a few of the things that you can find to enhance your music education program. The following sites provide a small sample.

**National Standards for Music Education**
http://www.menc.org

*MENC* is dedicated to the advancement of music education by encouraging the study and making of music. Online *MENC* journals and online news are just a few features of this music web site. The site also includes features such as the "100 Best Communities for Music Education" and discussion of musical career opportunities.

**Worldwide Internet Music Resources**
http://www.music.indiana.edu/music_resources/

This site is maintained by the William and Gayle Cook Music Library of the Indiana University School of Music. Visitors can link to any of the following topics:

- individual musicians (all genres) and popular groups
- groups and ensembles (except popular)
- composers and composition
- genres and types of music
- research and study
- the commercial world of music
- journals and magazines

**MusicNet**
http://www.thinkquest.org/library/cat_show.html?cat_id=17&cid=1

Within three main sections *(Encyclopedia, Professions,* and *Interactive)* of the *MusicNet* web site, visitors can learn about music education in a fun and educational manner. *MusicNet* features online games, message forums and real-time chat, a music encyclopedia with over 100 terms, and interesting music facts.

**Music Notes: An Interactive Online Musical Experience**
http://library.thinkquest.org/15413/

This site is designed to enhance music education for students of all ages. Topics include music theory, music history, and careers in music. Visitors can explore a variety of musical professions, learn how to read music, read about different instruments, and explore musical styles from Bach to Rock. A glossary and message board are also included.

**Piano on the Net**
http://www.pianonanny.com/

Students can learn how to play the piano by completing a series of lessons on the net. Each lesson takes about 35 minutes to complete. Students are encouraged to work slowly and at their own pace. Each lesson should be mastered before beginning the next.

**Classical Music Archives**
http://www.classicalarchives.com/index.html

The *Classical Music Archives* is the largest classical music virtual warehouse on the Web. The site offers tens of thousands of MIDI files in downloadable formats. The purpose of the site is to provide a central location on the Web where classical music is clearly catalogued for ease of use. The music of Beethoven, Bach, Chopin, and many others is available at this site.

# How Can I Use the Web to Find Information on Physical Education?

Physical education resources abound on the Web. The web sites are designed for teachers, parents, and students. Access to national requirements, assessment techniques, and lesson plans are but a few of the things available. The following sites provide a sample of physical education resources.

**National Standards for Physical Education**
http://www.aahperd.org/NASPE/publications-nationalstandards.html

The American Alliance for Health Physical Education Recreation and Dance (AAHPER) promotes healthy lifestyles through quality programs. This web site defines the national standards for a physically educated person. The definition includes five major focus areas, which together answer the question, "What should students know and be able to do?"

### President's Challenge—Youth Physical Fitness Program
http://www.indiana.edu/~preschal/

This web site provides information about the President's Challenge Fitness and Health award programs, including criteria and guidelines for special needs students, homeschools, and demonstration centers. Events and standards for each level of award are provided. Links to fitness related sites (report from the Surgeon General, *Physical Activity and Fitness Research Digest*) are also included.

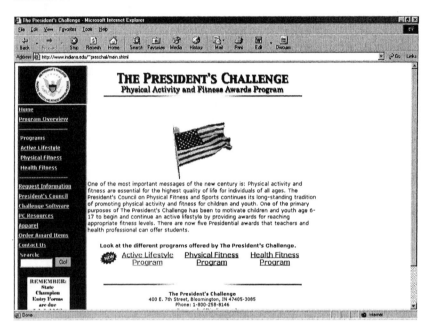

**PE Central**
http://pe.central.vt.edu/

*PE Central* is designed for physical education teachers, students, interested parents, and adults. The goal is to provide the latest information about contemporary, developmentally appropriate physical education programs for children and youth. Visitors are encouraged to submit their own lesson ideas that will be reviewed by the editorial board. The site includes links to assessment ideas, adapted PE lesson plans and equipment sources, cool web sites, health and nutrition ideas, and outdoor recreation activities.

*Summary*

The Internet and the World Wide Web are ideal resources for teachers and students who are interested in interacting with people, resources, and curricula at deeper levels than previously possible. Even though the resources listed in this section don't begin to represent all that is available, they provide a wonderful place to start. No matter what subject or what grade level you teach, you will find some of the best resources represented here. And if you're wondering how to begin, it's really quite simple. Just point your mouse and click!

# CHAPTER 5
## ACCESS TO HIGHER-ORDER LEARNING

*ISTE NETS IIIC: Teachers apply technology to develop students'*
*higher-order thinking skills.*

Most educators would agree that one essential goal of education is the development of students who are effective problem solvers. Although many schools have adopted the goal of developing students' critical-thinking and problem-solving skills, research indicates that these are not being addressed in the typical classroom. Teachers might not know where to begin to teach these types of skills in their classrooms. However, there are a variety of Internet sites you can use to promote the development of higher-order thinking skills in your students. These sites engage learners by challenging them to:

- think
- reflect
- discuss
- hypothesize
- investigative solutions
- make decisions
- compare results

Typically, these sites promote the development of higher-order thinking through the use of one or several of these approaches:

- Inquiry learning
- Interdisciplinary learning
- Critical thinking
- Problem solving

We realize that there is often a great deal of overlap among these approaches. For example, sites that promote interdisciplinary learning will also tend to promote critical thinking and problem solving. Our intent in this chapter is not so much to describe the unique aspects of each approach, but rather to highlight a variety of web sites you can use to address higher-order learning goals. What these sites have in common is an emphasis on student-centered learning experiences. Furthermore, almost all of these sites include an interactive component—one that requires students to make decisions and solve problems. As students interact with content, ideas, and each other they become meaningfully engaged in deep thinking about a variety of topics.

We begin this chapter by presenting information about these four approaches for promoting higher-order learning, including sample sites that illustrate each approach. Following this, we describe four different web-based activities that teachers can readily integrate into classroom lessons. We conclude the chapter with a list of sites that provide sample lesson plans for teaching the kinds of higher-order thinking skills described in this chapter.

## How Can I Use the Internet for Inquiry Learning?

Inquiry-based learning is a student-centered learning paradigm that emphasizes research, critical thinking, and multidisciplinary study to achieve course outcomes. Inquiry-based learning involves exploring the world, asking questions, making discoveries, and testing those discoveries in the search for new knowledge. It is complex, multifaceted, and has a variety of looks.

There are three main categories of inquiry-based learning: guided inquiry, student-directed inquiry, and student research. With guided inquiry, the teacher selects the topic and provides the materials for the students. Students design the exploration and analysis and then reach conclusions supported by their research. In student-directed inquiry, the teacher still provides the general topic, but the students are responsible for finding all materials. Under the student research model, the teacher provides support and guidance, while students handle all other aspects.

**Inquiry Learning Forum**
http://ilf.crlt.indiana.edu/

This site seeks to help teachers gain a better understanding of inquiry-based teaching and learning. In this forum, a teacher can

81

connect and interact with other teachers. Teachers also share inquiry-based lesson plans and resources. Finally, this site provides videos of inquiry-based experiments in classrooms.

**Concept to Classroom**
http://www.thirteen.org/edonline/concept2class/month6/

This web site provides a thorough description of inquiry-based learning. It describes a context for inquiry, the importance of using inquiry-based learning in the classroom, together with the application and outcomes of inquiry. The site also lists four essential elements for effective inquiry.

**Connect: Inquiry Learning**
http://www.exploratorium.edu/ifi/resources/classroom/connect/

This site describes the use of inquiry-based learning in the classroom, and provides research reviews and literature links. A section is included on using technology to support student inquiry.

**Inquiry Page**
http://inquiry.uiuc.edu/

*Inquiry Page* is a dynamic virtual community that discusses inquiry-based education. Resources and experiences are shared together with innovative approaches to this teaching style. The site is based on the John Dewey philosophy that education begins with the curiosity of the learner. The five components of inquiry (ask, investigate, create, discuss, and reflect) are described and discussed.

**Internet Innovations Incorporated**
http://www.biopoint.com/msla/links.html

This web site has many features not available in the other sites. Included are links to question development, where you evaluate the framework for developing effective questions for student research. Links to major search engines as well as methods to evaluate web resources are also included. Many links can be found on designing online instruction.

**Teach-nology**
http://www.teach-nology.com/currenttrends/inquiry/

*Teach-nology* claims to be "The Web Portal for Educators." In addition to classroom applications of inquiry, the site includes links to professional literature on inquiry. Games, a message board, list of best sites, tutorials, and teaching themes are also included.

## How Can I Use the Internet for Interdisciplinary Learning?

Interdisciplinary learning is supported by instruction that integrates a variety of traditional subjects. For example, developing curricula that are organized around a theme and that incorporate math, science, and the language arts would help create interdisciplinary instruction. As the National Council of Teachers of Mathematics (NCTM) describes, "Interdisciplinary instruction capitalizes on natural and logical connections that cut across content areas and is organized around questions, themes, problems, or projects rather than along traditional subject-matter boundaries. Such instruction is likely to be responsive to children's curiosity and questions about real life and to result in productive learning and positive attitudes toward school and teachers."
(http://www.nctm.org/about/position_statements/position_statement_14.htm)

According to Heidi Hayes Jacobs, President of Curriculum Designers Inc., "A curriculum that is interdisciplinary presents content, skills and thinking processes, and assessments through exploring connections among the disciplines."
(http://www.thirteen.org/edonline/concept2class/month10/)

Content
- topics, issues, themes, or problems that become subjects of learning

Skills and thinking processes
- developmentally appropriate benchmarks for students' learning, such as critical thinking, reading comprehension, analysis, math skill, etc.

83

Assessments
- products that demonstrate skills and thinking processes, such as essays, productions, recitals, projects, note-taking, and in-class participation, etc.

The following web sites provide additional information and examples of interdisciplinary learning.

**Concept to Classroom**
http://www.thirteen.org/edonline/concept2class/month10/demonstration.html

This web site provides an opportunity for you to take a video journey to see interdisciplinary learning in action in different classrooms. You can also visit web sites that showcase teachers' interdisciplinary work.

**AskERIC—Interdisciplinary**
http://askeric.org/cgi-bin/lessons.cgi/Interdisciplinary

This *AskEric* database includes over 75 interdisciplinary lesson plan examples for the K-12 classroom. Topics include water and soil erosion, Native Americans, coral reefs, apples, and much, much more.

**Interdisciplinary Learning Units**
http://www.nsa.gov/programs/mepp/msintdis.html

This web site offers a collection of interdisciplinary units collected over a six-year period. The units focus on middle school instruction and include *Roller Coaster Mania, Model Rocketry, Motion Magic,* and *Acid Rain.*

## How Can I Use the Internet to Promote Critical Thinking?

Critical thinking involves explaining, connecting, writing and rewriting, persuading, creating, deciding, and implementing. According to Anne Buchanan, critical thinking "is disciplined, self-directed thinking. It requires thinking about your thinking ... in

84

order to make your thinking clearer, more accurate and more defensible" (http://www.accessexcellence.org/21st/TL/buchanan/).

In order to promote critical thinking in the classroom, Buchanan suggests designing lessons around eight decision points:

- type of reasoning students will do (historical, biological, etc.)
- focus of the driving question, issue, or problem to be solved
- methods for capturing student interest
- types of grouping arrangements
- sequencing of lesson activities
- expected modes of student communication
- techniques for classroom management
- criteria and standards of assessment

For more information about the components of and strategies for teaching critical thinking, visit the web sites listed below.

**Critical Thinking Consortium**
http://www.criticalthinking.org

This web site is the home of the Foundation for Critical Thinking. Links are provided to events and resources (books, videos, and publications) that can help educators improve their instruction by incorporating critical-thinking skills. Sample "remodelled" lesson plans, in which critical-thinking components have been added to traditional lesson plans, are included for all levels: K-3, 4-6, 6-9, and 9-12. A link is included to the National Council for Excellence in Critical Thinking, currently consisting of 8,000 educators.

**Teaching Critical Thinking through Writing**
http://www.dartmouth.edu/~compose/faculty/pedagogies/thinking.ht ml

This site provides suggestions for developing critical-thinking skills in our students through the writing process. Even the simplest writing task, such as a summary of an article, requires students to make critical choices: "What information is most important to this argument?" "What might be left out?" More complex writing assignments require even more difficult choices about a topic—choices that eventually bring students to the questions: "What is it that I think about this subject?" "How did I arrive at what I think?" "What are my assumptions and are they valid?"

### Awesome Web Sites Evaluated by Kids – for Kids
http://istweb.syr.edu/AWArds/educators/index.shtml

Being able to evaluate web sites is an important skill for students today. This site was developed so that kids can become evaluators of the many web resources available to them for schoolwork, homework, and just for fun. Using a web evaluation tool called "Web Site Investigator," students explore the strengths and weaknesses of curriculum-related web sites. This site also helps teachers address the evaluation component of information literacy.

### DNA for Dinner
http://www.gis.net/~peacewp/webquest.htm

Here's a WebQuest lesson that promotes critical thinking among high school students by exploring the issue of genetically engineered foods. The task challenges students to draft a law that would address how to label genetically engineered foods in the United States.

### Critical Thinking for Primary and Secondary
http://www.criticalthinking.org/

The trend toward an emphasis on developing critical-thinking skills is one of the most significant changes in educational philosophy in the latter half of this century. This web site provides background articles, dialogue forums, guidelines, and lessons to help incorporate critical thinking into the curriculum.

### Number Watch
http://www.numberwatch.co.uk/

The author of this site, John Brignall, notes that this site is "All about the scares, scams, junk, panics, and flummery cooked up by the media, politicians, bureaucrats, so-called scientists and others who try to confuse you with wrong numbers." Students will also sharpen their critical-thinking skills by visiting related links including *Stephen's guide to logical fallacies* and *JunkScience.com: All the junk that's fit to debunk.*

## How Can I Use the Internet to Promote Problem Solving?

Problem solving involves cognitive effort directed toward achieving a goal when there is no obvious solution method known to the problem solver. According to Robert Harris (1998), a problem can arise from any of the following situations:

- an opportunity for improvement
- a noted difference between current and goal states
- the recognition of an imperfect present and a belief in the possibility of a better future (for more information visit: http://www.virtualsalt.com/crebook3.htm)

Problem-solving activities require students to apply higher-order thinking strategies and to synthesize knowledge from multiple curricular areas in order to solve given problems. Students refine their problem-solving skills as they make predictions, test hypotheses, manipulate data, and observe results and consequences.

**Sprocket Works**
http://www.sprocketworks.com/index.html

This interactive site uses Shockwave files to let you tour the night sky, play logic games, and learn how to groom a horse. Activities related to music, economics, science, art, and geography are included. This is one of those web sites where you cannot help but learn something.

**Access Excellence: The Mystery Spot**
http://www.accessexcellence.org/AE/mspot/

Find out what happened to the local frog population, explore Antarctica, or discover who's spreading disease in Two Forks, Idaho. The many activities included on this site are designed to allow you and your students solve mysteries using science.

**The Big6: Information Literacy for the Information Age**
http://big6.com/index.php

Developed by Mike Eisenberg and Bob Berkowitz, the *Big6* is a widely used approach for teaching information and technology skills. The *Big6* information problem-solving model integrates information "search and use" skills with technology tools in a systematic process to find, use, apply, and evaluate information for specific needs and tasks.

**The Geometry Center**
http://www.geom.umn.edu

Designed for use in both education and industry, this site provides links to geometry references, downloadable software, video and other course materials, and distance learning resources. Students can explore the effects of negatively curved space on a pinball-style game, examine a mathematical model of light passing through a water droplet in order to understand how rainbows form, or design a space station using geometrical principles.

**Illuminations**
http://illuminations.nctm.org

The *Illuminations* web site provides resources to improve the teaching and learning of mathematics for all students. Resources include interactive multimedia math investigations *(i-Maths),* video teaching vignettes, and a plethora of innovative lesson plans, all based on national mathematics standards. Complete *i-Maths* include student investigations, teacher notes, and answers. Both single- and multi-day lessons are included. Some of the multi-day *i-Maths* include video clips of teachers and students using the investigation, sample student work, assessment tasks, and related professional development activities.

## How Does Problem-Based Learning (PBL) Promote the Development of Problem-Solving Skills?

Problem-based learning (PBL) uses real-world situations or issues to encourage the development of critical-thinking and problem-solving skills, along with increased content knowledge.

PBL is characterized by:

- reliance on problems or questions to drive the curriculum
- use of ill-structured problems; there is more than one solution
- to any given problem
- student-driven problem solving; teachers serve as coaches only
- student-determined approaches to solving the problems
- authentic, performance-based assessment

PBL units begin with a "driving question" for students to solve or learn more about. Questions typically:

- are messy and incapable of being fully understood when first encountered
- change their nature as more is discovered about them
- defy solution by simple formula
- require careful consideration of the fit between solution and problem
- illustrate the difficulty of being certain one has the "right" answer because data can be missing or in conflict, even after extensive investigation

There are many Internet resources that both define and describe problem-based learning. In addition, many sites present sample units and problems that teachers can use in their own classrooms.

**IMSA Center for Problem-Based Learning**
http://www.imsa.edu/team/cpbl/cpbl.html

This site from the Illinois Mathematics and Science Academy provides a general overview of PBL, a comparison between traditional and PBL approaches, a list of ill-structured problems suitable for PBL investigations, and a number of model problems.

**UBUYACAR**
http://www.mcli.dist.maricopa.edu/pbl/ubuystudent/index.html

Part of Maricopa Community College's Problem-Based Learning site, this PBL manual for students starts with a problem statement:

"You are interested in purchasing a new vehicle. What should your annual salary be to afford the car you want?" Students are coached through the problem-solving process and are provided resources to help them solve this real-world problem. A *Tutor's Manual* coaches teachers in their roles as facilitators.

**Integrating Information Technology into Teaching**
http://www.usq.edu.au/users/albion/pblweb/

Created for preservice and inservice teachers, this site presents interactive problem scenarios that immerse teachers in the very real situation of trying to teach with technology. Visitors can view video interviews with teachers who use computers, access materials produced by those teachers, and visit additional web sites that deal with classroom uses of technology. This site offers a glimpse at the workings of PBL as well as ideas for incorporating technology into classroom-based learning activities.

About these materials | Using these materials | Acknowledgments | Copyright | Let's get started

Copyright (1999). University of Southern Queensland. Reprinted with permission.

# How Can I Use Web-Based Activities to Promote Higher-Order Thinking?

In recent years, a number of instructional activities have increased in popularity due to the ease with which the Internet facilitates them. These include both "old" activities such as scavenger or treasure hunts, as well as "new" activities such as WebQuests. In this section, we discuss four different types of web-based activities:

- Scavenger or treasure hunts
- Subject samplers
- WebQuests
- Collaborative projects

Although not necessarily focused on higher-order thinking skills, these activities can provide the foundation on which higher-order skills can be built. Each type of activity offers a relatively easy and fun way to integrate thinking skills into the curriculum.

## How Can I Use Scavenger or Treasure Hunts to Promote Higher-Order Thinking Skills?

Scavenger or treasure hunts are one way to use the Internet to promote higher-order thinking skills. A scavenger hunt includes questions for students to answer by visiting a variety of predetermined web sites that will provide the answer. This type of activity is a great way for students to practice problem solving, improve their reading, comprehension, and thinking skills, and learn how to search the Internet.

According to *Education World*, "Scavenger hunts, or treasure hunts, have quickly become one of the most popular tools for teaching students how to access and use the resources and information available on the Internet. There are many reasons for the hunts' rapidly growing popularity. Among them:

- Online scavenger hunts are easy to create and the resulting interactive searches are both fun and informative for students.
- The hunts can be geared to virtually any curricular area,

91

simultaneously providing students with technological and subject matter knowledge.

- Online scavenger hunts can be used as a whole-class activity, as a team activity, or as a means of providing individual students with review or enrichment activities.
- Scavenger hunts can be as simple or involved as circumstances dictate. Younger students may be provided with only a few questions, along with the links or URLs necessary for finding the answers, while older students may be given only a broad topic and asked to find their own sources for obtaining necessary information" (http://www.education-world.com/a_curr/curr113.shtml).

**Internet Treasure Hunts for Students**
http://www.ctnba.org/ctn/k8/treasure.html

This web site provides a collection of treasure hunts for K-12 students. A wide variety of topics are covered including poetry, Ancient Egypt, The California Gold Rush, and Colonial America. The *Collection of Hunts* section provides additional links where you can search by topic or curricular area.

**Adventures of CyberBee—Treasure Hunts**
http://www.cyberbee.com/hunts.html

This site offers a collection of treasure hunts centered on math, science, language arts, and social studies. You can use these treasure hunts to help discover web sites and find answers to some rather interesting questions like "How do you catch a bubble?"

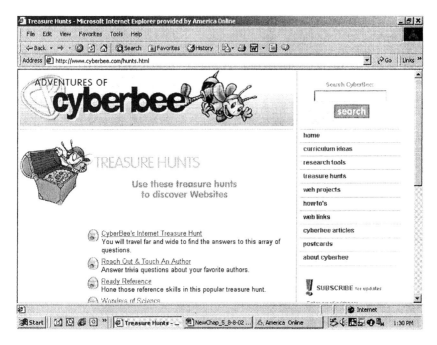

Copyright 1996-2002. Adventures of CyberBee. Reprinted with permission of the author Linda C. Joseph.

## Education World: Scavenger Hunts
http://www.education-world.com/a_curr/curr113.shtml

This web site provides a sampling of Internet scavenger hunts that have appeared on the pages of *Education World* during the past year. You can access a number of scavenger hunts including *Celebrate the Century, Black History, Animals of the World,* and *Track the Meteor Storm.* This site also provides a lengthy list of additional sources of Internet scavenger hunts and related articles.

## Scavenger Hunts for Kids
http://exit3.i-55.com/~vickib/hunts.html

Vicki Blackwell's *Internet Guide for Educators* provides information on professional development workshops and classes, upcoming events, and a newsletter. This Scavenger Hunt web page

93

is part of the *Blackwell's Best* link that includes multiple categories for finding help in integrating technology into your curriculum. Here you can explore scavenger hunts about *Greek Mythology, Alaska, Insects, Study Skills* and much more.

## How Can I Use Subject Samplers to Promote Higher-Order Thinking Skills?

The subject sampler is similar to a scavenger or treasure hunt in that it involves a guided search in which the web sites have been previously identified. The difference is that with the subject sampler, students are asked about their perspectives on topics, whereas with the scavenger hunt, students are asked to find specific, factual information. The subject sampler encourages students to compare their own experiences to the material presented, make interpretations, and respond in personal ways. This is a good way to get students connected to the topic and have them find value in the subject matter.

A list of strategies for creating a subject sampler follows:

- Create each component of the sampler activity including an introduction, activities on the topic, and a conclusion.
- Choose a topic for your sampler and write objectives.
- Search for web sites that contain information on the topic and the curricular objectives.
- Use the web sites to help generate questions for students to investigate and assignments for them to complete. Write questions using keywords from the specific web pages. These questions and assignments are the core of the activities.

Here are a few web sites that present information on subject samplers, along with examples that you can use in your classroom.

**Filamentality: Tips on Picking Links**
http://www.kn.pacbell.com/wired/fil/pick_links.html#Sampler

This web page includes general information on Subject Samplers, WebQuests, and Treasure Hunts with examples of each learning activity. This page will give you tips on the kinds of links that work

94

best depending on the goals you have for learners and the type of web page you are making. You will also find guidelines on searching for appropriate links and learn how to organize web-based resources by creating a "hotlist" or scrapbook.

**University of Richmond—Web-based Projects**
http://oncampus.richmond.edu/academics/as/education/projects/

Students, enrolled in "Integrating Technology Across the Curriculum" at the University of Richmond, have posted their web-based projects online. This web site is a collection of these students' subject sampler projects and includes examples on weather, inventions, women's history, and the Holocaust.

**The Connected Classroom: Strategies for Using the Internet**
http://www.qesnrecit.qc.ca/cc/inclass/sampler.htm

This web page introduces the concept of subject samplers and includes a template to help you create your own. There are also links to several subject samplers including *Ancient Egypt and You*, *Adventure with Huck Finn*, and *Pocahontas*.

## How Can I Use WebQuests to Promote Higher-Order Thinking Skills?

A WebQuest is a lesson plan that contains links to web sites that address a specific question, activity, or story. With a WebQuest, some or all of the information with which learners interact comes from resources on the Internet. This use of technology can enhance learning modules, while engaging students in the activities. Teachers can create WebQuests using either a WebQuest generating tool or word processing software. There are also many WebQuests available on the Internet that teachers can use in their classrooms.

Prior to 1995, the word WebQuest had yet to be invented. By 2002, there were over 750 sample quests included on the WebQuest page at San Diego State alone, with a daily hit rate of over 1700. Clearly the word is out; teachers are using WebQuests in their classrooms.

**The WebQuest Page**
http://webquest.sdsu.edu/webquest.html

This site is hosted by the Educational Technology Department at San Diego State University. It serves as a resource for instructors who use WebQuests in their classrooms. It has links to examples as well as training materials. You can find a multitude of examples at this web site. The matrix is divided by discipline and grade level.

**ISTE L&L Volume 26**
http://www.iste.org/L&L/archive/vol26/no7/features/yoder/

The history of WebQuests can be found here together with information on finding WebQuests or creating your own. Many links are provided that direct teachers to valuable resources.

**Kathy Schrock's Guide for Educators**
http://school.discovery.com/schrockguide/webquest/webquest.html

Kathy Schrock provides a list of links to WebQuest information. She includes links to exemplary WebQuests and a link to a form where you can submit your own WebQuests to share with others.

**TrackStar**
http://trackstar.hprtec.org

*TrackStar* helps teachers organize and annotate web sites that they want to use in a lesson plan. The web site list remains visible throughout the exercise, so students are able to stay on track. To find relevant WebQuests at this site, choose option "find a track" (e.g., search) with the keyword WebQuest.

## How Can I Use Collaborative Projects to Promote Higher-Order Thinking Skills?

Collaborative learning is based on the idea that the learning environment is naturally social. Students working on collaborative projects use common social skills to talk with other students in order to determine solutions to problems.

Having students work in a collaborative environment lays the foundation for relationships in their futures. Research has indicated that collaboration positively impacts student achievement. Not only do students learn the topic at hand, but they also learn the importance of working with, and learning from, others.

**Project Center**
http://www.eduplace.com/projects/

You can find or share collaborative projects on this web site. The projects include those for mathematics, science, reading and language arts, and social studies. *Project Center* also lists helpful tips for creating and posting collaborative projects to the Internet.

**CIESE Online Classroom Projects**
http://www.k12science.org/currichome.html

The Center for Improved Engineering and Science Education (CIESE) sponsors this helpful site that deals with online projects. The projects are designed to be interdisciplinary. Teachers from around the world can use the projects and resources found at this web site to enhance their curricula.

**Buddy[2]**
http://www.buddyproject.org/less/collab/default.asp

This site is designed to bring the collaborative project effort online. Students learn the basics of digital communication by joining or creating a collaborative project with other students. The four main components of the site provide information on how to prepare for collaborative projects, and develop, design, and deliver the resources.

**TERC**
http://www.terc.edu/

TERC is a not-for-profit education research and development organization that supports this web site with a multitude of ideas and resources. Among other exercises, students can experience real-life problems faced by NASA engineers. The TERC site provides news, resource links, as well as links to current and previous projects.

**Global SchoolNet (GSN) Internet Projects Registry**
http://www.gsn.org/pr/index.html

This site serves as a central warehouse for links to collaborative projects around the world. You can find projects hosted by GSN, as well as those from other reputable institutions. The site allows you to join an existing project or post one of your own.

**Collaborative Projects**
http://mathforum.org/workshops/sum96/data.collections/datalibrary/l esson.ideas.html

This web site lists dozens of past and current projects that you can use in your classroom. Many of the projects have been completed, but those can be used as models for your own efforts. Global water and temperature projects are combined with genetics projects to form a comprehensive list of ideas.

**Education World Collaborative Projects Community Center**
http://www.education-world.com/projects/

This *Education World* site provides featured projects of the week together with a large archive of projects. Projects are categorized by grade level and subject matter. A robust search engine allows you to easily find projects for your own specific needs.

**Loogootee Community Schools**
http://www.siec.k12.in.us/~west/online/join.htm

Teachers and students can easily join an online project from this web site. Projects include those in the sciences, language arts, and math areas as well as projects designed for critical thinking.

---

## How Can I Find Lesson Plans and Assessment Tools that Address Higher-Order Thinking?

Teaching and assessing higher-order thinking skills may present a challenge to teachers who have not focused on these skills before, or who have not had the opportunity to use the Internet for these purposes. In this section, we include links to some general resources for teaching higher-order thinking skills, as well as to a few sample lesson plans that can help you get started. For additional assessment ideas, refer to the rubric section in Chapter 3.

## Blue Web'n: A Library of Blue Ribbon Learning Sites on the Web
http://www.kn.pacbell.com/wired/bluewebn/

*Blue Web'n* is an online library of over 1200 outstanding Internet sites categorized by subject, grade level, and format (e.g., lessons, activities, projects, resources, references, and tools). You can search by grade level, broad subject area, or specific sub-categories (e.g., problem-solving, critical thinking). New sites are added each week.

## Mathematics Projects that Foster a Critical Look at Our World
http://www.enc.org/topics/inquiry/internet/document.shtm?input=FOC-001733-index

Using real-life investigations, Fanny Sosenke, a 7th grade mathematics teacher in Indianapolis, Indiana, motivates her students to critically examine the world around them and help them become quantitatively literate or "numerate."

## Sample Lesson: Teaching to Standards
http://gallery.classroom.com/34/116/amalven/amalven.html

This lesson, entitled *Third Grade Mystery Matchers*, helps students develop verbal, writing, viewing, listening, and problem-solving skills within a student-centered learning environment that emphasizes collaborative work, critical thinking, and informed decision making. Learning activities include opportunities for students to communicate using a variety of media and formats; to access and exchange information; to compile, organize, and analyze information; and to draw conclusions based on information.

## Why Should I Care about Rain Forest Deforestation: A Problem-Based Interdisciplinary Middle School Unit
http://research.soe.purdue.edu/challenge/RainForest/index.htm

This site, created by teachers at Tuttle Middle School in Crawfordsville, Indiana, effectively combines problem-based learning with an interdisciplinary focus to teach students about the rain forest. Links are provided to learning objectives, content standards, student activities and worksheets, assessment rubrics, and an extensive list of teaching resources.

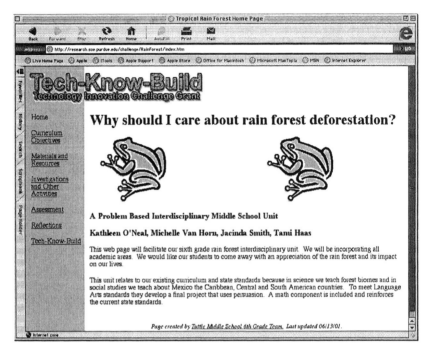

Copyright (2001) by the Tuttle Middle School 6th grade team. Reprinted with permission.

## *Summary*

The Internet is a powerful tool for developing and supporting students' higher-order thinking. Not only does it provide countless resources that describe these various approaches (e.g., inquiry-based learning, problem solving), but more importantly, it can provide the types of interactive content that are essential for successful use. The sites listed here give you a place to start in your own classrooms by providing specific teaching and assessment ideas for promoting higher-order thinking among your students.

# CHAPTER 6
## MAKING ACCESS EQUITABLE, SAFE, AND RESPONSIBLE

*ISTE NETS VI: Teachers understand the social, ethical, legal, and human issues surrounding the use of technology in PK-12 schools and apply that understanding in practice.*

As teachers start planning to use Internet resources in their classrooms, a number of issues arise that must be addressed immediately, even *before* access is obtained. These issues revolve around three main concerns: equity, safety, and responsibility. Teachers must assume primary responsibility for educating themselves and their students about all three areas of concern.

First, educators must help ensure that students have equitable access; that is, resources must be technologically and financially available to all students regardless of culture, gender, income, resources, or disability. Failure to provide equal access can lead to a growing gap between the information "haves" and "have-nots." Teachers must continue to make efforts to prevent inequity, which currently exists in many locations, from escalating.

The second issue relates to safety. Use of the Internet must not compromise students' safety. Although schools must help prevent students from being unnecessarily exposed to objectionable material on the Internet, students must also act to ensure their own safety by following both their school's guidelines, as well as the informal guidelines that govern online behavior (e.g., the rules of Netiquette). Achieving safe use requires that all users act appropriately, although, in reality, this does not always happen. According to Schrum and Berenfeld (1997), efforts are currently being made "to resolve these issues both politically and legally without challenging First Amendment rights" (p. 114).

The third issue relates to responsibility. When teachers and students use the Internet responsibly, they take care to evaluate the information that they access, to check for accuracy and value, and to give credit to those whose work they use. "Although there are laws and conventions to address traditional copyright infringements, plagiarism, privacy issues, document tampering, and individuals' freedom, similar conventions are rare in the world of digital information" (Schrum & Berenfeld, 1997, p. 117).

By discussing all of these issues with students *before* they access the Internet, many problems (although certainly not all) can be avoided. This section is designed to increase your awareness of the importance of each issue, as well as to identify ways to eliminate or manage the potential problems.

## What Does Equitable Access Mean?

One of the best things about the Internet is that it allows you to connect with people and resources around the world. One minute you can be sitting in your classroom in Coeur d'Alene, Idaho (http://www.sd271.k12.id.us/winton/), and the next minute you are on a virtual field trip to the Smithsonian Astrophysical Observatory in Cambridge, Massachusetts (http://cfa-www.harvard.edu/sao-home.html). Just a moment later, you are touring the National Museum of Science and Technology in Ottawa, Canada (http://www.science-tech.nmstc.ca/). It is almost as easy as snapping your fingers. Or is it?

Have you ever tried to connect with students in rural Arkansas? Although they might have computers, do they have access to the Internet? What if you want to connect with students in South Western Africa? They may not have access to telephone lines, let alone computers. How about connecting with students at the Colorado School for the Deaf and Blind? Can they truly receive the information that you have posted on your colorful, interactive web pages? As these examples have pointed out, not everyone enjoys equal access to these wonderful electronic resources. Not only is connectivity a problem in some areas of the world, but for special populations, access to these resources can be difficult if not impossible to achieve due to poor screen design, "untagged" images, poor navigational aids, and so on. If you ever intend to publish your resources and materials to the Web, these are important issues for you to consider.

## What is the Digital Divide and What Can I Do to Close it?

Although inequities still exist related to the availability of computers and Internet access among poorer schools and poorer countries, the access gap *has* started to close. However, teachers need to be aware of other gaps that persist despite the increasing numbers of computers in schools. These include disparities in access to high-quality technologies and "serious inequities in how technology is used for different groups of students" (Education Week, 2001, p. 12). When deciding how to use classroom computers with your students, be sure that girls, low achievers, low-income, and minority students all have equal opportunities (compared to boys, high achievers, well-to-do, and non-minority students) to use computers in ways that enhance their learning. When *types* of computer use become equal among groups, then the digital divide will truly begin to close.

## How Can I Make Web Resources Accessible to Special Populations?

People with disabilities (e.g., visual, hearing, motor, cognitive) deserve the same easy access to electronic information and resources as everyone else. For example, people with poor vision can benefit from web resources if web developers think to incorporate textual representations of their images and video files within their pages. Similarly, people with hearing impairments can benefit from textual representations of audio files. It takes but a little forethought during the development process to achieve a higher level of accessibility. Web developers (including you and your students) can find suggestions on the Internet that discuss how to make web pages more readily accessible to people with special needs. Some helpful web sites are included below.

**Webcast Series: Improving web accessibility for individuals with disabilities**
http://www.wiche.edu/telecom/projects/laap/webcast/webcast5.htm

This web site provides a general introduction to the topic of accessibility through a PowerPoint presentation by Cyndi Rowland, the director of *WebAIM* (Keeping Web Accessibility In Mind; http://www.webaim.org). A number of simulations are included that allow users to experience common accessibility errors such as those experienced by persons with visual, hearing, motor, and cognitive impairments. Suggestions are made for improving accessibility, and a number of electronic resources are provided.

**EASI: Equal Access to Software and Information**
http://www.rit.edu/~easi

*EASI* serves as a resource to the education community by providing information and guidance in the area of access-to-information technologies by individuals with disabilities. *EASI* stays informed about developments and advancements within the adaptive computer technology field and distributes that information to colleges, universities, K-12 schools, libraries, and into the workplace. *EASI* promotes equal access through on-site and online workshops, publications, videos, email discussion lists, an information-rich web site, electronic journal, and through participation in a wide variety of regional and national conferences.

**Center for Applied Special Technologies (CAST)**
http://www.cast.org/

The *Center for Applied Special Technologies* provides suggestions for making web-based resources available to people worldwide. According to *CAST*, these suggestions "are not 'workarounds,' nor do they require a sacrifice of design elements. Some are enhancements to traditional web sites, such as image and sound descriptions. Others are simply appropriate uses of common web design elements such as graphical navigation, tables, and the wording of text." Through the use of universal design elements, *CAST* advocates web sites that are useful, well designed, and universally accessible. The suggested design principles include:

1. ALT-tags and picture descriptions for all images
2. Text equivalent of all sound and video files
3. Graphical and textual representations of navigation system on all pages
4. Color coding of pages by the sections in which they are found for easy identification
5. External links open in new window
6. Index and "back to index" links

7. Text versions of tables
8. Text access (text links in addition to graphical links)
9. Inclusion of new html 4.0 accessibility tags (for more information see http://www.w3.org/wai/gl/)
10. Cascading style sheets

## *How can I determine if a web site is universally accessible?*

**Bobby**
http://bobby.watchfire.com/bobby/html/en/index.jsp

To determine if a web site is universally accessible, use *Bobby*, a web-based public service offered by CAST that analyzes web pages for their accessibility to people with disabilities as well as their compatibility with various browsers. To display the "Bobby Approved" icon, all pages on the web site must meet the requirements outlined in the guidelines above.

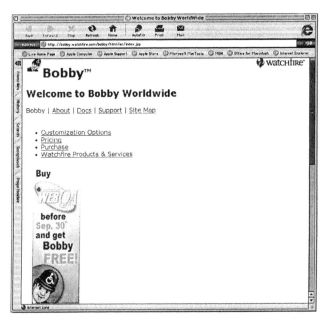

Copyright (2002) by Watchfire Corporation. All rights reserved. Reprinted with permission.

105

*How can I obtain web accessibility tools?*

**WebABLE!**
http://www.webable.com/

*WebABLE! Solutions* provides links to web accessibility tools including voice browsers and screen readers, as well as links to legal standards supporting accessibility. The mission of *WebABLE!* is to "stimulate education, research and development of technologies that will ensure accessibility for people with disabilities to advanced information systems and emerging technologies." This site also includes a database that lists hundreds of Internet-based resources related to accessibility.

**Microsoft Accessibility: Technology for Everyone**
http://microsoft.com/enable/default-u.htm

This site provides general information, as well as step-by-step tutorials, for adjusting accessibility features in Microsoft products to meet your specific needs and preferences. Information is also included about assistive technology products that work with computers that run the Windows operating system.

*How can I develop web-based lessons that are universally accessible?*

**Universal Design for Learning (UDL)**
http://www.cast.org/udl/UniversalDesignforLearning361.cfm

*Universal Design for Learning (UDL)* is a relatively new paradigm for teaching, learning, and assessment that draws on brain research and new media technologies to respond to individual learner differences. Links are provided that help users find and adapt digital content that is accessible to students with disabilities.

**Assistive Technology and the Multiage Classroom**
http://www.techlearning.com/db_area/archives/TL/2002/03/assistive.html

Authors Terry Lankutis and Kristen Kennedy note that while technology is an important part of the move toward inclusive classrooms, exploring new teaching models is equally important to creating effective learning experiences for all students—with and without recognized disabilities. Information is provided about promising technologies for meeting students' special needs, including tools that provide text-to-speech conversion, word prediction, and concept mapping.

## *How do I connect with people in other countries?*

Accessibility issues extend beyond the needs of special populations. Accessibility also relates to connecting with people in rural areas of the United States, as well as people in other countries.

### Intercultural E-Mail Classroom Connections (IECC)
http://www.iecc.org

*IECC* is a free service that helps teachers link with partners in other countries and cultures for email classroom pen pal and project exchanges. Since its creation in 1992, *IECC* has distributed over 28,000 requests for email partnerships. At last count, more than 7,650 teachers in 82 countries were participating in one or more of the IECC lists.

### Web66: International School Web Site Registry
http://web66.coled.umn.edu/schools.html

*Web66* maintains the Internet's oldest and most complete list of school web servers, including schools in Australia, Africa, Canada, Europe, and Japan. Visitors can search by level of school as well as by special categories such as *Parochial, Handicapped, Montessori, Gifted and Talented,* and *Online.*

## *Summary*

As you start creating your own web pages, it is important to keep in mind the issue of equal access. It does not take a lot of extra effort to assure that the web sites you develop are accessible to users who have physical or sensory limitations. Ensuring access for people in rural areas or developing countries will be more difficult to resolve. However, through an increased awareness of these issues, we can begin to consider ways to minimize access difficulties so that everyone has an equal opportunity to enjoy these rich resources.

## What Does Safe Access Mean?

As with print media, it is important to protect students from objectionable information. Because of the amount of information on the Internet, and the ease with which students can access it, assuring safety is a difficult task. Thus, several guidelines and U.S. laws are now in place to help protect children who use the Internet.

There are both formal and informal guidelines designed to keep students safe when using the Internet. Informal guidelines refer to the rules of proper behavior on the Internet. These are commonly known as Netiquette (Network Etiquette) and include rules such as:

- avoid abusive or foul language
- do not interfere with another person's email
- refrain from sending inappropriate messages
- avoid typing in all caps . . . IT SEEMS LIKE YOU'RE SHOUTING!

To learn more about Netiquette visit http://www.albion.com/netiquette.

Formal guidelines, referred to as Acceptable Use Policies (AUPs), and U.S. laws regarding the Internet are discussed below.

### What is Acceptable Use on the Internet?

Because Internet access is now common within our schools, a clear set of guidelines is needed. These guidelines, or AUPs (Acceptable Use Policies), are used to guide proper use of the Internet by students, teachers, administrators, parents, and board members. An AUP needs to specifically state what type of Internet use is acceptable, and what steps will be taken if the Internet is used in an unacceptable manner. Day and Schrum (1995) define an AUP as "a written agreement signed by students, their parents, and their teachers outlining the terms and conditions of Internet use..."

There are two primary reasons for creating a school AUP:

- to protect children and adolescents from inappropriate material
- to protect the school system from litigation

Day and Schrum devised a checklist of issues that an AUP must address (1995, p. 9). These guidelines include:

- define the Internet in simple terms
- outline the Netiquette rules that students must follow
- address ethical and legal issues, including copyright laws
- define objectionable material in the same manner used by current media selection policies for printed material
- stress that Internet access is a privilege, not a right
- clearly establish the penalties and consequences for abuse of Internet privileges

The web sites below address these issues as well as others. Samples of AUPs can be viewed and adapted to your specific needs.

**Houston Independent School District's Acceptable Use Page**
http://chico.rice.edu/armadillo/Rice/Resources/acceptable.html

The Texas Studies Gopher began collecting Internet AUP resources a number of years ago and now provides a large number of links to a variety of AUP articles, studies, and sample forms. These resources will provide Internet guidance for students, teachers, administrators, and board members.

**Acceptable Use Policies: A Handbook**
http://www.pen.k12.va.us/go/VDOE/Technology/AUP/home.shtml

The Virginia Department of Education has created a handbook of acceptable use policies. The handbook provides links to sites with information on the components of an AUP, sample school/division AUPs, samples and templates for an AUP, and other resources.

**Internet Acceptable Use Policies.K12**
http://falcon.jmu.edu/~ramseyil/netpolicy.htm

This site is a collection of web sites with information for educators who are writing district acceptable use policies. Links to AUP articles and samples from several states including Texas, Minnesota, California, and Indiana are provided.

## What U.S. Laws Govern Our Use of the Internet?

Over the past several years, three U.S. laws—Children's Online Privacy Protection Act (COPPA), Children's Internet Protection Act (CIPA), and the Family Educational Rights and Privacy Act (FERPA)—have gone into effect to ensure the safe use of the Internet and to help protect the privacy of students. Although some of these laws are being contested based on the First Amendment right of free speech, it is still critical for educators to check school policies related to these laws. The following web sites provide additional information on each of these laws.

**Children's Online Privacy Protection Act (COPPA)**
http://www.ftc.gov/ogc/coppa1.htm

The Children's Online Privacy Protection Act became effective on April 21, 2000. This law addresses the online collection of personal information from children under 13. The new rules delineate what a web site operator must include in a privacy policy, when and how to seek verifiable consent from a parent, and responsibilities for protecting children's privacy and safety online.

**How to Comply with the Children's Online Privacy Protection Act (COPPA)**
http://www.ftc.gov/bcp/conline/pubs/buspubs/coppa.htm

The Federal Trade Commission staff prepared this guide to help you comply with the new requirements for protecting children's privacy online and understand the FTC's enforcement authority.

### Children's Internet Protection Act (CIPA)
http://www.ifea.net/cipa.html

The Children's Internet Protection Act went into effect on April 20, 2001. This new law places restrictions on the use of funding that is available through the Library Services and Technology Act, Title III of the Elementary and Secondary Education Act, and on the Universal Service discount program known as the E-rate (Public Law 106-554). These restrictions take the form of requirements for Internet safety policies and technology that blocks or filters certain material from being accessed through the Internet.

### Complying with the Children's Internet Protection Act (CIPA)— FAQs
http://www.dpi.state.wi.us/dpi/dlcl/pld/cipafaq.html

The Wisconsin Department of Public Instruction web site has summarized the CIPA law and provides answers to frequently asked questions regarding compliance issues.

### Family Educational Rights and Privacy Act (FERPA)
http://www.ed.gov/offices/OM/fpco/ferpalist.html

The Family Educational Rights and Privacy Act originally went into effect in 1974 to protect the privacy of student education records. This act gives parents certain rights with respect to their children's education records. Since the Internet has made the sharing of information much easier, this law has received new attention regarding the sharing of student files and records via the Internet. This web site provides an overview of the FERPA and includes links to a fact sheet, regulations, and legislative history.

### How Can Schools Block Access to Offensive Sites?

In addition to an AUP and U.S. laws, schools can use special software to protect their students and staff from accessing questionable information on the Internet. Running monitoring and blocking software designed to disallow access to offensive material can prohibit exposure to unacceptable web sites.

The three web sites below link to software that can be used to filter information found on the Internet.

**Net Nanny**
http://www.netnanny.com/home/home.asp

*Net Nanny* filtering software protects children from questionable material on the Internet. It also can prevent information from going out onto the Internet, such as address, phone number, or other personal and sensitive data.

**SurfControl**
http://www.surfwatch.com

*SurfControl* helps organizations in every industry to manage content risk by offering a total filtering solution. Their products include both web and email filtering software to help protect students from harmful and obscene material online.

**Webroot**
http://www.webroot.com/chap1.htm

*Webroot* has released two new products—WinGuardian and ChildSafe—to help monitor use of the Internet. ChildSafe helps parents protect their children from the dangers of the Internet and can be used to block offensive or dangerous web sites, limit computer access, and email out logs so you can supervise your children from work or anywhere else.

*Summary*

The potential for harm to users and the legal liability of school districts are important issues related to the use of the Internet in the K-12 environment. School systems have to justify the worth of their Internet access investment by encouraging productive use of computing resources and discouraging negative or non-productive use of expensive computing and telecommunications systems. A formal policy of use, including consequences of misuse, can help define and monitor Internet access.

Monitoring and blocking software, such as the three listed above, are available to help parents and school systems protect impressionable children and adolescents from the darker sides of the Internet, such as pornography and hate speech.

## What Does Responsible Access Mean?

The Internet has quickly blossomed into a valuable source of information. The value of the information found on the Internet should often be questioned, however. Because the Internet is public domain, there are no restrictions on the type of material that can be posted on any web site. There are no editors or filters for evaluating the information. As a result, information found on the Internet may not always be accurate or credible. *Anyone* can post *anything* on the Internet.

It is the responsibility of the user to evaluate information gathered from the Internet for its accuracy and worth. Responsible users critically read Internet material, acknowledging the subjectivity of any information gathered from the Internet. Teachers and students should follow proper procedures for citing any Internet resources that they may use. As a liable Internet user, these steps are essential to follow to support responsible access.

### How Can I be Sure that Internet Information is Accurate?

Guidelines have been developed to help you critically evaluate web sites but even these guidelines are not yet standardized. To assure that the Internet information you receive is valid, it is wise to consider these guidelines along with your own assessment of "good" versus "bad" information. Remember that just because something is in print, it doesn't mean its accuracy is guaranteed.

Some basic questions to guide your evaluation include:

- Authority
  Who is the author of the piece? What experience does he/she have? What are his/her credentials?
- Affiliation
  What organization or institution supports this author? Is this a personal web site (proceed with caution) or is the material part of an official site?

- Bias
  Is the web site objective?  Does the organization have a political agenda?
- Currency
  When was the information created or last updated?  Are the links up-to-date?
- Content
  Are there errors in spelling and grammar?  Is the information logical?  Does the author include citations or a bibliography when facts or quotations are used?

All information, whether in print or on screen, needs to be critically evaluated by the reader for its credibility and accuracy.  These guidelines provide a basic framework for the evaluation of web-based material.  They are by no means complete.  For more help on evaluating the credibility and value of web sites, visit the addresses below.

**Kathy Schrock's Guide for Educators**
http://school.discovery.com/schrockguide/eval.html

This site offers ready-made, easy-to-use web site evaluation surveys for the elementary, middle, and secondary school levels.  It also includes links to other sites on critical evaluation of Internet resources.

**WWW Cyberguides**
http://www.cyberbee.com/guides.html

This site provides criteria for teachers to use in evaluating content and design of web pages.  It includes a guide for rating the curricular content on web sites and for rating the design of a web site.  It also includes the *Website Investigator,* an instrument for elementary students to evaluate web sites.

**Blue Web'n**
http://www.kn.pacbell.com/wired/bluewebn/rubric.html

*Blue Web'n* offers an evaluation rubric for assessing the quality of web pages.  It includes key categories and suggestions for scoring.

**Sites that Discuss Evaluating Web Sites**
http://www.lib.mankato.msus.edu/staff/smith/w3evalbm.html

This Minnesota State University web site includes several links to other sites that address credibility and evaluation of Internet resources.

### How Do Copyright Laws and Fair Use Guidelines Apply to Use of Content Found on the Internet?

Although a number of sites allow you to use their information without asking permission, an increasing number of authors are requiring permission to use their written work or graphic images. Most authors are more than willing to grant permission. However, understanding some basic copyright laws and fair use guidelines will help ensure that both you and your students are using Internet resources legally.

Copyright laws protect the author of original works. This protection gives the owner of the copyright, the author, exclusive rights to reproduce or distribute the work and to authorize others to do the same. The copyright laws that we normally associate with print also apply to the use of audio, video, images, and text on the Internet. Because the Internet is so accessible, it is much easier to copy and use images, text, video, and other graphics that are likely to be protected by copyright. Even if a document or graphic does not state that it is copyrighted, it is a good idea to assume there is a copyright. By understanding the laws, you can avoid copyright violations and use copyrighted materials legally. If you are unsure about the legal use of a document, you always have the option to ask for permission from the copyright holder. Note that the authors of this text received copyright permission to use the screen shots included in this book.

Fair use guidelines define the limitations on the exclusive rights of the copyright holder, the author. Typically, educators and students have unwritten permission for limited use of documents or graphics for educational purposes and for a limited time. Determining fair use is not always easy; you should be knowledgeable about the basic copyright and fair use guidelines and policies for educators.

The following web sites can help you become more familiar with copyright laws and fair use guidelines for both print and graphics.

**Copyright Resources on the Internet, Groton Schools**
**http://groton.k12.ct.us/mts/pt2a.htm**

This Groton Public Schools web site provides an extensive number of resources on copyright laws and fair use guidelines for the K-12 educator. This web page includes resources for both copyright and acceptable use policy and ends with an A to Z list (by state) of K-12 policies and guides.

**UMUC Information and Library Services**
http://www.umuc.edu/library/copy.html

This University of Maryland College web site provides a number of links to sources on copyright and fair use in the classroom, on the Internet, and the World Wide Web. The resources provide an introduction to copyright and fair use, fair use guidelines, and a sample letter to request copyright permission.

**Work4Women Multimedia Gallery**
http://www.work4women.org/multimedia/howtouse.cfm#obtain

This web site includes information on receiving permission to copy and use an image or video that you find on the web. Sample permission language is provided to help you create your own permission request form.

### How Do I Cite Information from the Internet?

The purpose of any citation is to lead the reader to all sources used by the writer. Both teachers and students should be aware of the procedures for correctly referencing Internet sources. This is not a simple chore as there are many kinds of materials to be referenced, as well as a variety of acceptable citation styles.

Currently, three predominant styles exist for citation of material found on the Internet—The American Psychological Association (APA), The Modern Language Association (MLA), and Chicago Style. Because there are so many variations on the kind of information you can gather from the Internet, it is best to consult the individual web sites for examples of how to cite a particular electronic reference.

**Online! A Reference Guide for Using Internet Resources**
http://www.bedfordstmartins.com/online/citex.html

This web site provides information on citing electronic resources using APA, MLA, Chicago styles and more.

**APAStyle.org**
http://www.apastyle.org/index.html

This site contains information on citing electronic media and URLs, and citations in text of electronic materials.

**OWL: Online Writing Lab**
http://owl.english.purdue.edu/handouts/research/r_mla.html

Purdue University's *Online Writing Lab* offers information on the Modern Language Association (MLA) format and other citation methods. Examples of citations for both print and electronic sources are provided.

**The Chicago Manual of Style**
http://www.chicagomanualofstyle.org/

This web site offers answers to frequently asked questions regarding the Chicago citation style. Questions and answers are grouped by keyword with additional links to related web sites.

*Summary*

The Internet offers a wealth of information, much of which is neither monitored nor edited. As a result, the user must be responsible for evaluating materials found on the Internet. Internet users should filter material from the Net with questions on its accuracy, value, and quality. Proper citation of Internet sources is also necessary. Users are obligated to give credit to those whose work they use. In short, it is the responsibility of the user to follow appropriate steps and procedures that guarantee responsible access.

Integrating the Internet into your classroom offers both significant challenges and amazing benefits. If you are just starting to use the Internet you may feel a little anxious about trying to learn all there is to know. However, our advice to you is to simply jump in and get started. The sooner you begin, the sooner you and your students will benefit from the many resources and learning opportunities offered through the Internet. You may not have, nor may you *ever* have, all the right equipment or all the necessary knowledge, but by opening your door to the possibilities of the Internet, you and your students come one step closer to becoming a WorldWide Classroom.

## *References*

Day, K., & Schrum, L. (1995). The Internet and Acceptable Use Policies: What schools need to know. *The ERIC Review*, 4(1), 9-11.

Education Week. (2001, May 10). Technology counts 2001: The new divides. *Education Week, 22*(35). Retrieved March 11, 2002 from http://www.edweek.org/sreports/tc01

Schrum, L., & Berenfeld, B. (1997). *Teaching and learning in a telecommunications age: A guide to educational telecommunications.* Needham Heights, MA: Allyn and Bacon.

# GLOSSARY

**Acceptable Use Policy (AUP).** An agreement signed by teachers, students, parents, and school administrators that contains a definition of the Internet, a description of use that is acceptable, and a list of steps that will be taken if the Internet is used in an unacceptable manner.

**Ask an Expert.** Web sites to which you can post questions and receive answers from qualified "experts" (e.g., teachers or professionals). Answers are usually received in a few days or less.

**Bookmark.** A list of URLs saved within a browser. The user can edit and modify the bookmark list to add and delete URLs as the user's interests change. Bookmark is a term used by Netscape, while Favorites is the term used by Explorer.

**Browser.** A software program that is used to view information on the Internet.

**Browser hand.** An icon that appears when you move the mouse over a link (text or image).

**Bulletin Board Service (BBS).** An electronic bulletin board. Information on a BBS is posted to a computer where many can dial in and read it and comment on it. BBSs may or may not be connected to the Internet. Some are accessible by modem dial-in only.

**Chat mode.** A form of online discussion in which messages are exchanged in real time.

**Chat room.** A real-time environment that allows a group of people to type messages that are seen by everyone in the "room."

**Children's Internet Protection Act (CIPA).** This law restricts the use of funding available through a number of government acts. These restrictions take the form of requirements for Internet safety policies and technology that blocks or filters certain material from being accessed through the Internet.

**Children's Online Privacy Protection Act (COPPA).** This law addresses the online collection of personal information from children under 13.

**Clickable image (hot spot).** An interface used in web documents that allows the user to click or select different areas of an image and link to another web page or a specific area on the current web page.

**Collaborative projects.** Instruction in which groups of students work together toward a common goal. Students learn the importance of working with and learning from others.

**Collaborative workspaces.** Files on a computer network that can be accessed by all members of a group; allows members to share work or information.

**Copyright.** The exclusive legal rights to reproduce, publish, or sell the content of a piece of work.

**Critical thinking.** Disciplined, self-directed thinking that involves explaining, connecting, writing and rewriting, persuading, creating, deciding, and implementing.

**Database.** A file or collection of files that contains records of similar information or data.

**Dead link.** A URL that is no longer available on the Internet. Clicking on one of these links results in an error message.

**Digital divide.** Inequities regarding the availability of computers and Internet access among poorer schools and poorer countries.

**Discussion groups.** A form of asynchronous electronic communication among several people. Participants connect with others via the Internet to share advice or gather information on topics of interest.

**Domain designator.** Tells what kind of group owns the server. Examples: com = business; edu = school; gov = government agency; mil = military agency; org = organization.

**Domain name**. The unique name that identifies an Internet site. The naming convention for domain names is two or more parts separated by dots (periods).

**Download**. The process of transferring a file, document, or program from a remote computer to a local computer.

**Email**. The short name for electronic mail. Email is sent electronically from one person to another. Emails also can be sent to many different people at the same time by using a mailing list.

**Email address**. The location to which an email is addressed. It includes the user ID, the "at" sign, the domain name, and an extension.

**Equitable access**. Equal access to high quality Internet technologies for people in any country, economic situation, or with any type of special need.

**Fair use guidelines**. Define the limitations on the exclusive rights of the copyright holder.

**Family Educational Rights and Privacy Act (FERPA)**. This act gives parents certain rights with respect to the distribution of their children's educational records.

**FAQs (Frequently Asked Questions)**. A file or document where a moderator or administrator will post commonly asked questions and their answers. If you have a question on any web site, it is usually best to check for the answer in FAQs first.

**Favorites**. See Bookmark.

**Filtering software**. Software that a school installs on its computer networks that prevents access to sites with inappropriate content. Can also be used to keep track of the time spent on any web site.

**Firewall**. Software that a school installs on its computer networks that block access to sites with inappropriate content.

**Forums**. Forums are "spaces" or areas where messages are posted on an electronic bulletin board for anyone to read and respond to.

**FTP (File Transfer Protocol)**. A procedure used to transfer large files and programs from one computer to another. Access to the host computer may or may not require a password.

**GIF (Graphics Interchange Format)**. A format created by CompuServe to allow electronic transfer of digital images.

**Home page**. A web document that is the initial or start-up page shown when a web site is accessed.

**Hot links or hot spots**. Elements within a document (text or graphics) that are used to link to another item or web page.

**HTML (Hypertext Markup Language)**. The most common language used to write documents that appear as web pages on the World Wide Web.

**HTTP (HyperText Transport Protocol)**. The common protocol used to communicate between World Wide Web servers.

**Hyperlink**. Elements within a document (text or graphics) that are used to link to another item or web page.

**Image**. A graphical representation on a web page that can be used as content, as navigation, or as a link.

**Inquiry-based learning**. A student-centered learning paradigm that emphasizes research, critical thinking, and multidisciplinary study to achieve course outcomes.

**Instant Messaging (IM)**. Communication technique that allows you to maintain a list of people with whom you wish to interact. You can send messages to any of the people on your list, as long as that person is online.

**Interdisciplinary learning**. Instruction that integrates a variety of traditional subjects (e.g., curricula that are organized around a theme and that incorporate math, science, and the language arts).

**Internet.** A network of millions of computers that are connected worldwide.

**IRC (Internet Relay Chat).** A channel is created and users log on to the channel. Anything that is typed is seen by everyone on the channel.

**ISP (Internet Service Provider).** An organization that provides access to the Internet.

**Java.** A computer programming language frequently used for web development.

**JPEG (Joint Photographic Experts Group).** A commonly used graphical file format used to transfer digital images.

**Links.** Elements within a document (text or graphics) that are used to link to another item or web page.

**Listserv (Mailing list).** A list of users who have subscribed to the service. A single email message can be sent at once to the entire list of people.

**MIDI (Musical Instrument Digital Interface).** MIDI files use the .mid file extension. These types of files contain instructions rather than sounds. They are used to transmit information via a digital interface to an FM synthesizer or a wave table device.

**MPEG (Motion Picture Experts Group).** A format used to make, view, and transfer both digital audio and digital video files.

**National Educational Technology Standards (NET*S).** Standards that define broad areas of technology competency for students; developed by the International Society for Technology in Education (ISTE).

**National Educational Technology Standards (NETS*T).** Standards that define broad areas of technology competency for teachers; developed by the International Society for Technology in Education (ISTE).

**Netiquette (Network Etiquette).** Informal guidelines that govern proper behavior on the Internet.

**Newsgroups.** Discussion groups that can be on the Usenet and are established for sharing similar interests or discussing related topics. Newsgroups are "spaces" or areas where messages are posted on an electronic bulletin board for anyone to read and respond to.

**Plug-in.** A program that works within a larger program to add additional capabilities to the usability of a software tool (e.g., the Flash plug-in for multimedia presentations). Plug-ins may have to be downloaded to utilize advanced features of a web site.

**Portfolio.** An assessment technique in which samples of students' works are collected and stored.

**Problem-based learning (PBL).** Instruction that uses real-world situations or issues to encourage the development of critical thinking and problem-solving skills, along with increased content knowledge.

**Problem solving.** Cognitive effort directed toward achieving a goal when there is no obvious solution method known to the problem solver.

**Publishing.** The process of uploading web pages to a web server.

**QuickTime.** A format used by Apple Computer to make, view, edit, and send digital audio and video files.

**Responsible access.** The responsibility of the user to evaluate information gathered from the Internet for its accuracy and worth.

**Rubric.** A printed set of scoring criteria that helps a teacher evaluate students' work.

**Safe access.** Protecting students from objectionable information on the Internet.

**Scavenger or treasure hunt**. Includes questions for students to answer by visiting a variety of predetermined web sites that will provide the answer.

**Search engines**. Programs on the Internet that categorize information in databases and retrieve that information in the form of searches.

**Signature**. Information posted on the bottom of a web page that generally indicates the last date of modification and the party responsible for the maintenance. A signature can also be used at the bottom of an email to identify the sender.

**Site map**. An at-a-glance guide to the contents of a web site.

**Streaming audio and video**. Hearing sounds or seeing action on the Internet. Streaming technology sends images and sounds a little at a time, rather than downloading entire files completely, which is time consuming.

**Subject sampler**. Similar to a scavenger or treasure hunt, students are asked about their perspectives on specific topics.

**Tag**. An HTML command used to mark, or specify the format of, the text that is to be displayed on the web page.

**Telementoring (Tutoring)**. Web sites with an array of qualified experts that can help answer your questions. These experts may be teachers or professionals in the area you are researching.

**Telnet**. The process of remotely connecting to and using a computer at a distant location.

**Threaded discussion board**. An informal meeting place in which communication occurs among people who are posting messages to a common software program. All participants are required to have access to the same software program.

**Upload**. The process of moving or transferring a document, file, or program from one computer to another computer.

**URL (Uniform Resource Locator)**. An address used by people on the Internet to locate web pages. The address includes the protocol used for information transfer, the host computer address, the path to the desired file, and the name of the file requested.

**Usenet**. A world wide system of discussion groups. Usenet contains over 10,000 discussion areas, called newsgroups.

**Web-based video conferencing**. Also called a classroom conference, this is a virtual meeting conducted over the Internet in which the participants can see and hear each other, even though the attendees may be in different places.

**Web page**. A document that you view in your browser (e.g., Internet Explorer, Netscape). The document can fill one screen or multiple screens, giving the user the ability to scroll to view it all.

**WebQuest**. An inquiry-oriented activity in which some or all of the information that learners interact with comes from resources on the Internet.

**Web server**. A software program used to provide, or serve, information to remote computers. Web pages can be "published" to a web server.

**Web site**. A group of web pages that are created and maintained by a group or individual. Web pages in a web site generally serve the same purpose.

**World Wide Web (WWW)**. A subset of servers on the Internet that use HTTP to transfer hyperlinked documents in a page-like format.

**WorldWide Classroom**. A classroom that evolves as educators learn to integrate Internet resources into meaningful curriculum-based learning experiences. A WorldWide Classroom connects teachers and learners to rich resources available through the Internet.